J.R. LANDER is Professor Emeritus of History at the University
of Western Ontario, and the author of numerous books.
Among them are *Conflict and Stability in Fifteenth Century Eng-
land; Ancient and Medieval England: Beginnings to 1500;* and
Government and Community: England, 1450–1509. Professor
Lander now lives in London, England.

Recent scholarship in late medieval and early modern government has begun to explore the vast differences between the
intentions of legislation and the realities of the administration
which resulted from it. In these essays J.R. Lander analyses
the actual workings of government as distinct from the aspira-
tions of the statutes.

In the minds of both political thinkers and the political
nation the functions of government were limited to defence
and to the maintenance of justice, with few or none of the
positive 'welfare' activities of the modern state. Subjects were,
on the whole, adamantly opposed to any extension of government activity which would cost them money. The government,
therefore, had to work within these psychological limitations.
Practically it had to work with limited finances – operating
without proceeds of direct taxation to which there was intense
and successful resistance. To some extent the monarchy tried
to counteract these weaknesses by propaganda – by emphasis
on the theocratic nature of kingship, by the increasing splendour
of the ceremonial of the court, through architecture and
portraiture, and through pamphlets and chronicles. But, as
Lander demonstrates, in the end English government remained insecure and limited, with the internal peace and good
order of the kingdom precarious indeed.

THE
LIMITATIONS
OF ENGLISH
MONARCHY
IN THE LATER
MIDDLE AGES

The 1986 Joanne Goodman Lectures

J.R. LANDER

University of Toronto Press
Toronto Buffalo London

© University of Toronto Press 1989
Toronto   Buffalo   London
Printed in Canada

ISBN 0-8020-5807-8 (cloth)
ISBN 0-8020-6724-7 (paper)

Printed on acid-free paper

Canadian Cataloguing in Publication Data

Lander, J. R. (Jack Robert), 1921–
   The limitations of English monarchy in the
   later middle ages

   (The 1986 Joanne Goodman lectures)
   Includes index.
   ISBN 0-8020-5807-8 (bound)   ISBN 0-8020-6724-7 (pbk.)

   1. Great Britain – Politics and government –
   1066–1485.   2. Monarchy – Great Britain – History.
   I. Title.   II. Series: The Joanne Goodman
   lectures; 1986.

   JN137.L35 1989   320.94203   c88-094435-8

The Joanne Goodman Lecture Series

has been established by Joanne's family

and friends to perpetuate the memory of her

blithe spirit, her quest for knowledge, and

the rewarding years she spent at the

University of Western Ontario.

Contents

Preface

I should like to thank Mr E. Goodman and his family, and the trustees of the Joanne Goodman Lectures, for doing me the honour of inviting me to return to the University of Western Ontario, where I spent so many happy years, for this occasion. I should also like to thank Mr Goodman and the trustees for their generosity in making possible the publication of these lectures.

J.R. Lander
London, England

Choir of St George's Chapel, Windsor

The gates of Edward IV's tomb,
St George's Chapel, Windsor

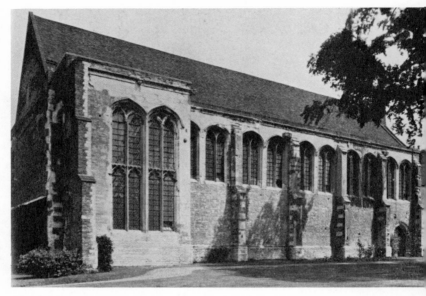

Eltham Palace

Detail of ironwork,
Windsor Castle

Henry VI

HENRICVS VI·D·G·ANGLIÆ ET FRANCIÆ REX DOMINVS HIBERNIÆ ET c

HENRY the VI borne at Windſor being of the age of eight Monthes.
beganne his reigne the 31 of Auguſt 1422. and crowned King of
England at Weſtminſter the 6 of Nouember 1429. and of Fraunce
the 7 of December 1432. he reigned 38 yeres 6 monthes, he died by
violence, May 21. aged 52. Año 1471. firſt buried at Chertſey Abbey, thence
remoued to Windſore, wher he was ſolembley interd .

R E ſculpſit

Edward IV

Henry VII

The half angel or angelet of Henry VI,
struck at Bristol 1470/1

1

Government
Finance
and War

IN THE LAST THREE CHAPTERS of Book v of his famous *Mémoires*, Philippe de Commynes painted a most depressing picture of fifteenth-century monarchy, and, in particular, of French monarchy, depicting it, more or less, as a system of tyranny, with kings surrounded by sycophants and flatterers, oppressing their subjects, particularly in matters financial, for their own benefit alone, and so unrestrained by any mortal sanctions that in the final resort they were controlled only by the inscrutable justice of God.[1] Only God was powerful enough to restrain princes: and he frequently intervened in their affairs – a theme to which Commynes returned time and time again with an almost obsessive fascination.[2] Sir John Fortescue in his *De laudibus legum anglie*, written in exile in that country, reached more or less the same conclusions about France under its system of absolute government, or *dominium regale*,[3] and there, and also in *The Governance of England*, vividly contrasted with it the liberty and prosperity of English subjects under their less tyrannical system of *dominium politicum et regale*.[4] In particular he drew a memorable contrast between the grinding poverty of the French peasantry and the prosperity of their English counterparts: a contrast amply substantiated by French sources themselves. The cahier of the third estate of the Estates-General held at Tours in 1484 describes the French peasantry as so ruined by war taxation and the brutalities of royal troops billeted upon them that many

are dead of hunger in great and uncountable numbers: and others out of despair have killed wives, children and themselves seeing that they had nothing on which to live. And many men, women and children, for lack of beasts, are forced to labour, yoked to the plough.[5]

In England we have only complaints of villages depopulated to make sheep runs[6] and the nineteenth-century pioneer economic historian, Thorold Rogers, could show the fifteenth century in England as a golden age for the peasant, the artisan, and the labourer.[7]

The contrast is interesting and to a great extent true, though one might point out that Commynes in a pessimistic way was concerned to depict realities, in particular French realities, while Fortescue in the *De laudibus* gave an idealized picture of how English government, in his opinion, ought to have worked. As he was well aware, its actual practice was riddled through and through with violence and corruption; yet though, as everybody knows, in *The Governance of England* he was extremely critical of the workings of government under Henry VI, even there his prejudice in favour of English institutions is obvious enough. However, in both books, Fortescue was above all concerned to praise the limitations under which English kings traditionally laboured: limitations from which he supposed their people significantly benefited.

'Limitations,' in these lectures, will be used in two senses: theoretical restrictions, more or less generally assumed by contemporaries, upon the powers of monarchs, and practical restrictions tacitly imposed upon their exercise of power by the nature of the contemporary political and social structure. As for political speculation, during the late fourteenth and the fifteenth century the general dearth in England of much theoretical writing or theoretical *justification* for kingship may well be surprising to those accustomed to sixteenth-century adulation of the mighty prince. It almost appears that, seeing no practical alternative to monarchy, Englishmen viewed it unenthusiastically as one of the inevitable facts of life and were more concerned to stress its possible shortcomings than to glorify its potentialities.

In day-to-day affairs, by twentieth-century standards, the aims of the late medieval and the early modern state were distinctly limited – negative and disciplinary. Positive aspects such as communications, health, education, social welfare, which loom so large in the activities of the modern state, fell completely outside the scope of government in this period.

The king's office, as Fortescue remarked, citing the first book of

Kings,[8] 'stondith in ij thynges, on to defende his reaume ayen þair enemyes outwarde bi the sworde: an other that he defende his peple ayenst wronge doers inwarde bi justice.'[9] The Tudor chronicler, Edward Hall, writing in the 1540s, put an imaginary speech in the mouth of Archbishop Arundel (1353–1414) which, with equal clarity, shows the very limited objectives of contemporary government. If government functioned as it ought, he said, 'then the noble men shall triumph, the rich men shall live without fear, the poor and needy persons shall not be oppressed nor confounded':[10] sentiments which more or less continued to prevail until the end of the *ancien régime*.[11] Even in the late eighteenth century Edward Gibbon remarked in *The Decline and Fall of the Roman Empire,* in phrases remarkably similar to those of Edward Hall, that the functions of government were 'to protect the fortunes of the rich and to do justice to the poor.' Social and political attitudes were, therefore, totally different from those of modern times. The most that men expected from government was that it would not allow public order to fall below a certain rather vaguely understood threshold. The natural corollary was they were not prepared to pay for any wider functions. Government was therefore caught in a vice of limiting traditional sentiments and restrictive finance.

Such traditional sentiments were based upon a more or less tacit consensus: one of those assumptions so general that they were rarely put into words. Limitations, in fact, stretched even further than the above remarks imply because private people by virtue of their local standing and their property performed vital services which we nowadays associate only with public bodies. In the countryside, peers and the higher clergy and gentry acted as justices of the peace, the lesser gentry and more prosperous farmers as hundred bailiffs. In the towns, burgesses did their tours of duty as constables. The higher a man's position in the social hierarchy and the greater his wealth perhaps the greater was his responsibility in local government. Private property and public activity were inextricably intermingled. Government was a function of property and property rights were to a great extent the foundation of even the royal foreign policy.

This extreme emphasis on property rights carried with it an equally extreme emphasis on law: a lawyer's rather than a politician's view of government. By Fortescue's time at least, if not considerably earlier, men felt that, rather than parliament, the mass of technical rules and practices protecting their property was the fundamental safeguard of English liberty when contrasted with what they saw fit to regard as French slavery. It was above all the duty of a strong and well-endowed monarch to uphold this complicated corpus of property rights.[12]

To deal first with external relations: with the exception of the German free cities and the Italian city republics (which were, of course, giving way at this time to tyrannies), the kingdoms of Europe based their external policies upon the principles of dynasticism. Although, in the minds of sophisticated clerical, and even some lay, thinkers, kingship was an office to be exercised for the good of the subject, in practice men regarded kingdoms as 'livelodes,' as inheritances, and the sanctity of the inheritance was one of the very strongest of contemporary sentiments. An estate (and, therefore, a kingdom) was not so much the property of an individual as a sacred family trust to be handed down intact from generation to generation and, if possible, increased.[13] The political unit was basically a form of property to be acquired and added to by inheritance, marriage, and even purchase, and in the last resort to be defended and extended by warfare[14] waged with the support of two sections of the people – a small minority who took an active part in campaigns, lured by the prospect of booty and the attraction of possible land grants in conquered territories, and the much larger section of the population which owed an obligation, deeply rooted in feudal custom, to support their lord with financial aid as the more active minority supported him with their bodies and their arms. Internally, as we shall see later, in spite of a superficially impressive network of public institutions, particularly judicial and financial institutions, the coercive sanctions necessary to maintain public order derived more from local men of property than from the powers of officials appointed by the central government.[15]

The main theoretical limitations on the English monarchy, which at the same time resulted in severely practical restrictions, were in the fields of legislation and finance. From the reign of Edward I onwards parliament had gradually, but firmly, imposed its partnership upon the monarchy in both areas. By the middle of the fourteenth century it was well established that law could be made and repealed only by statutes and that statutes could be made only by the king in parliament – a principle firmly reiterated by Sir John Fortescue as one of the twin pillars of his famous theory of *dominium politicum et regale*[16] – in firm contrast to the powers of the king of France, who could legislate through his own unimpeded will, the *dominium regale*.[17]

The opinion that practical restrictions may well have become more rigid during the fifteenth century than in earlier periods is well illustrated by the history of the royal finances. In the twelfth century, for example, royal exactions had been arbitrary in the extreme. In 1198, when Richard I was preparing for a new forest eyre to mulct his people, Roger of Hoveden complained that 'the itinerant justices had just reduced all England from sea to sea to destitution when another kind of torment was begun by the justices of the forest to the confusion of all men.'[18] The financial oppressions of the thirteenth-century eyre were, and are, notorious. Royal exactions increased as government grew more efficient. After Edward I introduced a new system of personal taxation, its results during two decades of continuous war or preparations for war reduced some of his poorer subjects to such grinding misery that they were forced to sell their seed corn in order to pay their taxes.[19] Mercifully, no such extreme complaints were ever heard in the fifteenth century. During the fourteenth-century stage of the Hundred Years' War, as Sir Goronwy Edwards pointed out, the commons became reasonably generous with their financial demands.[20] At the same time, G.L. Harriss has convincingly demonstrated the degree of control which they developed over grants. Traditionally the commons were obliged to support the king's necessity, but they established their right to be the judges of that necessity, and Edward III always had to make out a good case for his war demands.[21] Moreover, royal demands for taxation were undoubtedly less in this period than they had been earlier because Edward III's armies were very much smaller than those which Edward I had raised and so were less of a crushing burden on the community.[22]

Even so, Englishmen became successfully and adamantly resistant to realistic tax assessments. By 1334 the Edwardian system of personal taxation, the fifteenth and tenth (a tax on moveable property, a kind of primitive capital levy, rather than an income tax), was already so swamped by evasion and corruption, conventional valuations, and fraudulent underassessments that its yield was reduced by almost two-thirds.[23] It was then standardized at this low level, which bore little relationship to the wealth of the country. The government abandoned the previous practice of assessing individuals each time the tax was levied. In 1334 each district (county, city, or borough) was allotted a quota and left to raise the sum as it chose. Further reductions, extorted from the government, followed in the mid-fifteenth century.[24]

By the late fifteenth century Edward IV was raising no more than an average of £10,700 a year from direct taxes on personal property. Henry VII did a little better with about £12–13,000 a year. Both kings also raised an average of about £12,000 a year from benevolences. On top of this Edward took over £7,000 a year and Henry about £9,000 a year from the clergy.[25] The out-of-date assessments for these taxes, both lay and clerical, were notorious enough for comment by the Venetian ambassador in 1497.[26] By 1500 direct taxation contributed only about one-fifth of the royal income.

Serious decline also affected indirect taxation, the customs system. During the thirteenth and fourteenth centuries English wool, the highest-quality wool in Europe, was essential to foreign weavers, especially those of Tuscany and Flanders. The government was, therefore, able to impose an export tax at the enormous rate of about 30 to 33 per cent. From the 1340s English cloth manufacture, with some marked fluctuations, steadily expanded, absorbing more and more of the native wool crop. English cloth, though good, was not of the highest quality. Taxation at the same enormous rate as that of wool would have priced it out of foreign markets. The export tax on cloth, in fact, was a mere 3 to 5 per cent of its value. The switch from the export of raw wool to the export of manufactured cloth, though beneficial to the English economy, was something of a fiscal disaster for the government.[27] Moreover, all through the fifteenth century the government was convinced that the customs system was riddled through and through with corruption.[28] Although Edward IV and Henry VII manfully tried to reduce evasion and cheating, they remained rampant enough, and neither king ever dared to make a direct attack upon the current ludicrously low valuations.[29] Even after the famous Book of Rates of 1507, which in any case seems to have been applied only in the port of London, the assessment of goods remained unsatisfactory and their valuation for customs purposes entirely conventional, in some cases as low as one-seventh of the true commercial value of the goods concerned.[30]

There was, of course, a long tradition, hallowed by the opinion of no less a saint than Thomas Aquinas, that direct taxation should be levied for extraordinary purposes only, the most common of which was war.[31] Although most people followed the saint, some grudged even this. The Welsh extremist, Adam of Usk (writing in the 1420s), declared that God had cast his righteous judgment in the defeat of Sir John Arundel's naval expedition of 1379 because it had been impiously financed from the proceeds of taxation[32] and in the last remaining section of his *Chronicle* he sanctimoniously hoped that Henry v would not suffer the fate of tyrants like Caesar, Asshur, Alexander, Hector, Cyrus, and Maccabeus in divine retribution for the enormous sums of money which he had wrung from wretched victims of all classes to pay for the conquest of his 'Norman inheritance.'[33]

Amongst the tax-paying classes in general, such attitudes hardened, if anything, as the century wore on. An experiment with a graduated income tax on all freehold land and offices worth more than £5 a year in 1436, owing to significant underassessment, realized no more than £9,000.[34] Edward iv's attempts between 1472 and 1475 to impose new forms of taxation to pay for war against France proved an utterly humiliating fiasco. The lords, who made a separate grant of their own, underassessed themselves in the most brazenly impudent manner.[35] The commons surrounded their grant of an income tax with the most galling restrictions. The money collected was to be placed in special repositories and not to be released to the king until the commons gave special permission. The assessments went wrong or were infinitely delayed, some of the collectors embezzled part of the money they had gathered in, and more was stolen from the special repositories. In the end the king had to fall back on the traditional, totally out-of-date, underassessed fifteenth and tenth, and with infinite personal exertion had to supplement this with a benevolence from his subjects – that is, a personally solicited gift from anybody the king thought capable of making a contribution – an immensely time-consuming process for the king himself and for those of his prominent servants also involved in cajoling or bullying contributions out of reluctant subjects. This was surely an extreme form of institutional atavism: a rather desperate return to the conditions of the thirteenth century before Edward I had evolved the system of collective consent to taxation by representatives of the local communities in parliament.[36] In 1489 Henry VII met with even more spectacular financial disasters. Parliament and the two ecclesiastical convocations between them voted £100,000 for war with France. No more than £27,000, possibly as little as £20,000, was ever collected.[37]

Far worse, people even resisted the cost of defence. In 1408 the commons argued that the heriditary Lords Marcher alone, by virtue of their tenure of land, should bear the cost of defending the Marches of Wales against Welsh insurgents,[38] and in 1497 the men of Cornwall and the south-west rose in revolt, producing the most dangerous crisis of Henry VII's reign, rather than pay taxes for the defence of northern England against the Scots, taxes which their own representatives in parliament had assisted in voting.

Such attitudes meant that from the 1470s until well into the reign of Henry VIII the kings of England just could not afford an aggressive foreign policy which involved anything like prolonged campaigning.[39] They were emasculated by the financial outlook of their subjects – a restriction which accounts for the caution, even the timidity of Edward IV and Henry VII in their foreign relations – a timidity for which Edward IV in particular has been most unrealistically and unfairly castigated by historians who have failed to take into account his extreme financial weakness.[40]

The result of this retreat from taxation was, as B.P. Wolffe has so convincingly demonstrated, an emphasis from the 1380s upon the principle of endowed monarchy, the idea that 'the king should live of his own,' his own being in the eyes of his subjects principally the profits of the crown lands and the proceeds of the customs system. Calls for the king 'to live of his own' grow louder and louder, stronger and stronger, reaching a climax in 1449 to 1450 when the house of commons vociferously demanded an act of resumption, that is the repossession from grantees of all crown estates, offices, and pensions, so that by a reduction of its patronage, the direct management of its lands, and a more equitable distribution of offices the crown could exploit its estates for the maximum cash advantage. As we shall see later, the demands of patronage and the maximization of income were the somewhat incompatible functions of the crown lands and it was always extremely difficult for any government to maintain a nice balance between them. After 1461 Edward IV, wise in his generation, adopted these opposition demands as official policy and the system of endowed monarchy quickly grew to maturity.[41]

These attitudes, of course, received their best-known contemporary expression in the works of Sir John Fortescue, in particular in *The Governance of England*. Generations of commentators have pointed this out, and it may well seem that there is nothing new to say on the subject. Commentators, however, have unfortunately tended to parrot each other on the subject rather than go back to Fortescue's text for themselves. Now, a careful reading of Fortescue's text reveals an obsessive, almost pathological, horror of direct taxation, particularly of its results as he had observed them during his years of exile in France with Margaret of Anjou.[42] More fundamental, and less noticed, however, was his own very peculiar conception of the nature of the royal endowment. His support for the policy of resumption and the creation of a new endowment for the monarchy which should be inalienable was nothing new or startling.[43] As I have already mentioned, the idea of endowed monarchy had been steadily gaining ground since the 1380s and the idea of the inalienability of the royal resources seems to have been commonplace enough since at least the thirteenth century.

What, however (so far as I know), has been completely overlooked is that Fortescue's own views were so unusual, so extreme, so completely alien to our modern ways of thought that he compared the king of England to a pious founder and the kingdom itself to the greatest of perpetual chantries, that is an institution with a fixed and permanent endowment for the singing of masses for the soul of the founder or founders. The relative passage is so odd in the context of government finance that it deserves quotation *in extenso*. Fortescue wrote that once the king had resumed his 'lifelode' it should be 'amortised' and never again alienated without the consent of parliament

wych than wold be as a newe ffundacion of is crowne, he shall be þerby the grettest ffounder of þe world. Ffor þer as other Kynges have ffounded byshopriches, abbeys, and oþer howses of relegyon, þe Kyng shall þan have ffounded on holl reaume, and endowed it with gretter possescions, and better then euer was any reaume in cristendome. This maner of ffundacion mey not be ayenste þe Kynges prerogatyf, or his liberte, no more than is þe ffundacion off an abbey, ffro wich he may take no parte of the possescions wich he hath onis geve hym, with owt þe assent off þer covent. But this maner off endowment off his crowne shalbe to þe Kyng a gretter prorogatyff, in that he hath then enriched is crown with such riches and possescions, as never Kyng shall mowe take from it with out þe assent off is holl reaume – And trewly, yff the Kyng do thus, he shall do þerby dayly more almes, þan shall be do be all the ffuncdacions þat ever were made in England. Ffor euery man of the lande shal by this ffundacion euery day be the meryer, þe surer, ffare þe better in is body and all his godis, as euery wyse man may well conseyue. The ffundacion of abbeys, of hospitals, and suche other houses, is nothyng in comparisoun herof. For this shalbe a collage, in whiche shul syng and pray for evermore al the men of Ingland spirituel and temporel – .[44]

No more than a fantastic literary conceit, you may be tempted to think. But I am not so sure that this particular passage can be so easily dismissed. The very serious chief justice was not a particularly imaginative man and he did not indulge in fantasies. Fortescue seems to have been totally serious in making this comparison.

In any case the system of endowed monarchy, whether or not we see it as a gigantic perpetual chantry, was not in the event conspicuously successful. As I have written elsewhere, the period 1450 to 1509 presents something of a unity in the field of English government finance: a period which saw the popular beginnings of the system, its growth to maturity, and the development by 1509 of a resentful backlash against what some people regarded as its excesses.[45] By 1509 the descendants of the generation of the 1450s which had demanded the rigid conservation of the royal endowment were excoriating Henry vii for his rapacious exploitation of the system. He had upset the nice balance of the twin purposes for which, in their opinion, the system should have been exploited – patronage and cash revenue. Henry viii, immediately upon his accession, found it wise to relax his father's methods, with a disastrous reduction of the cash flow. Like many an abbey the great perpetual chantry of England found it difficult to maintain and defend its endowment in a highly acquisitive society in which voracious seekers after patronage were often hardly distinguishable from predators.

This weak financial structure affected the powers and the activities of government in every direction. The English monarchy could afford nothing like a standing army, a police force, or an extensive bureaucracy. While the French as a result of the Hundred Years' War were developing permanent forces, a small standing army, the English still raised their wartime forces through what is best described as private armies – the indenture system. The only permanent levies were the garrisons of Berwick, Carlisle, and Calais,[46] which obviously could not be used as a field force, and such somewhat sporadically organized royal bodyguards as Richard ii's notorious force of Cheshire archers, Edward iv's guard of two hundred archers hastily recruited during a political panic in 1468,[47] and Henry vii's fifty to two hundred yeomen of the guard.[48] In 1497 Raimondo De' Raimondi, the Milanese ambassador, noted with surprise the very small military establishment,[49] lack of fortresses, and lack of arms of the English monarchy. Moreover, corruption was very high amongst such forces as were called together for the few short campaigns of the late fifteenth century. Military stores and equipment quickly vanished in the most alarming manner.[50] In preparation for overseas campaigns the king made contracts, drawn up in legal indentures with members of the nobility and gentry, to supply mixed contingents of men-at-arms and archers. Such contingents varied from as many as a thousand or more raised by a royal duke or two hundred or so by a baron to a mere half-dozen or less provided by a country gentleman.[51] The king paid the contingent leaders at a standard rate at the Exchequer and they, in turn, paid their followers. Even the war-mongering Henry v had to rely on this system, and, as Maurice Powicke has demonstrated, by this time, owing to declining enthusiasm for foreign war on the part of a large proportion of the aristocracy and gentry, neither Henry nor his successors were ever able to develop a really large corps of experienced commanders. Under Henry v himself, as early as 1417 to 1422 only 31 out of 177 of the contingent leaders were veterans of the Agincourt campaign of 1415, and even of this remnant of 31 only 25 went on to serve in the armies of Henry vi. Long before the final French recapture of Normandy in 1450 and of Guienne in 1453 in England the idea of a military career was distinctly *passé*.[52] This diminished enthusiasm was also accompanied by a marked decline in the quality of such English armies as were assembled for foreign service. By the 1470s they contained far too large a proportion of archers as compared to men-at-arms. They had no knowledge of siege warfare. Recruited as they were for *ad hoc* occasions, they were almost useless at the beginning of a campaign,[53] and as more than one continental writer derisively observed they were far too fond of their creature comforts in the field.[54] Again, in the second half of the fifteenth century writers such as William Worcestre and William Caxton saw fit to deplore the declining martial spirit of the English gentry and their increasing preoccupation with civilian affairs.[55] K.B. McFarlane thought that the English aristocracy had already become the most civilian in Europe, pointing out that even by the early fifteenth century the crown promoted men to the peerage more for their contributions to government than for war service.[56]

At this time continental war was a matter of chevauchées, devastation, and long-drawn-out sieges. By contrast the English civil wars, the so-called Wars of the Roses, were a matter of short sharp campaigns. For example, in 1485 the campaign (if we can really dignify it by such a grand term) which ended in the decisive battle of Bosworth Field lasted for exactly fourteen days. The armies taking part were small untrained levies hastily collected for these particular occasions and equally rapidly disbanded. None of the protagonists could afford anything better or more permanent.[57] Moreover, evidence is accumulating that many even of these troops were forced into the field against their wills. The author of 'Gregory's Chronicle' claimed that in 1450 Jack Cade terrorized 'alle the gentellys' of Kent to revolt with him.[58] In 1459 veteran soldiers brought by the earl of Warwick from Calais refused to fight against Henry VI at Ludford.[59] In 1461 Margaret of Anjou threatened with death those who did not respond to her call to arms.[60] Warwick did the same in 1471. In the same year the Bastard of Fauconberg also recruited by intimidation in Kent.[61] Polydore Vergil wrote that in 1483 the duke of Buckingham's forces against Richard III consisted of Welshmen 'whom he, as a sore and hard dealing man had brought to the feild agaynst their wills, and without any lust to fight for him.'[62]

Cities and towns would make considerable efforts for their own defence, but not to answer a royal summons. A threatened French attack on Yarmouth in 1457 roused Norwich, a score or so miles up the River Yare, fearing for its own safety, to muster and equip a force of 600 men to assist in the defence of its neighbour, but in 1461 an appeal by Henry VI produced only 120 – and this from what was then probably the second largest city in the kingdom. The contributions to the Wars of the Roses of lesser towns like Ipswich and King's Lynn rarely exceeded twenty men.[63]

To sum up, England, though far from an orderly country by modern standards, escaped the devastating wars which afflicted continental countries. The taste of the nobility and gentry for continental campaigns to support the dynastic claims of their rulers to foreign territory was distinctly limited. Furthermore, because the country was part of an island with only one land frontier, that against Scotland, the demands of defence were far, far less urgent than elsewhere. The English political nation, therefore, became withdrawn and insular – in their safety from attack and aggression less military, more civilian in character, and able, unlike continental subjects, to deny the monarchy an adequate taxation base. The monarchy struggled in vain with this limitation until the middle of the seventeenth century, so much so that the opposition politicians of the 1620s lived in the same financial thought-world as those of the late fifteenth century and government finance did not achieve a modern footing until the period of the Commonwealth and the Restoration.

2

Central and
Local
Government

EVEN FOR THE SAME GROUPS OF PEOPLE, statistics compiled in different ways from varying sources can be confusing and misleading. In using them it is generally wise to make allowances for more or less considerable margins of error. However, for Canada in the year 1973 about 2.2 million men and women or about 20.4 per cent of the total labour force is a reasonable figure for those employed in the public sector. Some of these were in the armed forces, some employed in local government, and many, many more in education, health, and other social services. Those who in traditional language would be classed as 'civil servants,' men and women directly employed in administrative, executive, clerical, and various minor capacities, amounted to something over 100,000 people – that is about one in every 240 of the country's population.[1] By these standards what one might call the 'civilian bureaucratic establishment' of late medieval England was very small indeed – at the most not more than one civil servant for every 1,050 of the population. Moreover, their functions were by no means exactly comparable, as about two-fifths of these were employed in the law courts, so that we can plausibly reduce the figure to one for every 2,070 of the population.[2]

To investigate the actual distribution of these civil servants, their total number nominally at the direct command of the king can hardly have exceeded 1,500 men – perhaps 250 to 300 knights, esquires, yeomen, and pages in the politically significant section of the royal household, perhaps 100 in the Exchequer, 150 in the Chancery, about the same in the law courts and about 30 or 40 receivers and auditors staffing the new Yorkist system of estate management and financial control centred in the King's Chamber, 80 or 90 customs officials[3] and about 700 or 800 local keepers of royal parks, castles, and forests and stewards of royal manors.[4] Each county had its sheriff's office and its staff in a large county like Lincolnshire could number up to 100. These appointments, however, were in the control of the sheriff, not the king, and, whatever had been the case earlier, by the mid-fourteenth century the sheriffs' offices had become notorious centres of corruption.[5] Many of the local offices, allotted mainly to local gentry, if not sinecures, as an unknown proportion of them certainly had become, were mostly concerned with the exploitation of royal rights and were used as much for political patronage as for the effective enforcement of government policies. Through these offices, together with the establishment of the royal household, the government established a wide affinity of its own, a useful communications network in the countryside. The 60 esquires of the household were 'to be chosen of men of theyre possession, worship and wisdom: also to be of sundry sheres, by whom it may be knowne the disposition of the countries.'[6] They did stints of duty turn and turn about, three months at court and three months in their own localities. As the Second Anonymous Croyland Continuator wrote, Edward IV

took care to distribute in all parts of the Kingdom custodies of castles, manors, forests and parks so that no man however powerful he was in any part of the realm could attempt anything without his knowing.

As a system of espionage and control, intermingled as it was with the affinities of the magnates, it was obviously better than nothing, but after all it was not a system of independent bureaucratic control. At best it was no more than a method under which the local *potentiores* were set spying upon each other. Operating as it did as a form of patronage, it was also limited by aristocratic competitive demands for the exercise of royal patronage. Sir John Fortescue noted:

And this hath causyd mony men to be suche braggers and suytours to þe kyng, ffor to haue his offices in þer contraes to thaym selff, and to þer men, þat almost no man in some contray durste take an office of þe Kyng, but he ffirst had þe good will off þe said bragers and engrossers of offices. Ffor yft he dyd not so, he shuld not affir þat tyme haue pease in his contray; whereoff hath comyn and growen mony gret trowbels and debates in dyueres contraes of England.[8]

His words are amply confirmed by other evidence. Local aristo-crats expected to control many such offices, by demanding direct royal grants either to their own nominees, or to themselves, after which they appointed deputies to carry out the duties, thus increasing their own local influence at the expense of the royal coffers.[9] Under Henry VI pressure of this kind in certain areas of the country, as Fortescue remarked, had reached the level of intimidation. Thus royal patronage was seriously diluted by powerful local interests.[10]

Restrictions applied in other ways too. The gradual, but increasingly rapid, change from clerical to lay civil servants in the central departments of government was not entirely a form of progress, as historians once supposed. Clerical civil servants could more easily be got rid of, as dismissal did not spell the loss of the incomes which they derived from ecclesiastical benefices. Laymen resented dismissal far more for it often meant the loss of a considerable part of their revenues. They, therefore, more and more demanded life tenure of offices and even reversion to their sons. The development of a lay bureaucracy meant a loss of control and a valuable degree of flexibility.[11]

Nor did such civil servants as there were command tools which we take for granted today. By modern standards the lack of information available to governments was staggering. Even information which they possessed was often for practical pur-poses inaccessible. By the fifteenth century the English govern-ment had accumulated extremely voluminous archives but their form (they were generally kept in cumbersome rolls) and the lack of any effective indexing system meant that much of the information which they contained could not be effectively used, though during the fifteenth century, particularly in the Yorkist period, greater efforts do seem to have been made in this direction. The Lancastrian Exchequer produced frequent, possibly even annual, estimates of royal financial needs and resources and by Richard III's time the government had drawn up comprehensive lists of local offices and was better informed about these than ever before.[12] Even so, however, there was something of a strange inhibition about using in an effective way some of the information which was available, and the commons were particularly hostile to governmental retention of any new information upon the taxable capacity of the country.[13] They tried to insist on the destruction of the records of any experiments in raising revenue.[14]

At the top of the social scale there were between 50 and 60 peerage families: immediately below them were the gentry, which an informed guess would put at about 6,500 families in 1500. Of these perhaps 2,000 were major figures in their county communities, a minority of them differing very little in wealth and status from the lesser members of the baronage.[15] From their ranks the king chose the sheriffs and the majority of the justices of the peace. In view of their acknowledged importance, I find it surprising that so little is known about the fifteenth-century justices.[16] Technically, of course, they were officials appointed by the crown, but to regard them, for that reason, as the equivalent of modern officials is to be guilty of the most serious and unrealistic type of anachronism. After all, the coercive power necessary to enforce their decisions and judgments came from their local landed wealth and their influence over their tenants and lesser neighbours. It is generally assumed that apart from a ceremonial sprinkling of peers and a stiffening of lawyers they were always local men.[17] This was true in the main, though I am beginning to have some reservations about it. Certainly the government's choice was limited to the extent that political opponents were rarely long excluded from the county commissions. One political mistake did not spell permanent disgrace.

The area of choice was limited and the influence of local men was too valuable for that to happen.[18] Moreover, government intrusions into local spheres of influence led to the most serious political resentment: this certainly happened under Henry vi, particularly during the period of Suffolk's ascendancy, in Wales and the Marches, areas where the duchy of Lancaster estates were widespread, and particularly in south-eastern England and the home counties, as vehement complaints from Kent at the time of Cade's rebellion testify.[19] Again A.J. Pollard has demonstrated that a southern tradition exceedingly hostile to Richard iii, a tradition which condemned him as a tyrant, derived from the fact that he forced noted northern 'foreigners' into southern county communities, lavishly endowing them with estates forfeited under the attainders which followed Buckingham's rebellion and putting them into key local offices and onto commissions to the exclusion of local families who considered such positions as theirs by hereditary right.[20] Pollard has amply proved his case, but I hope to show in my forthcoming book on the justices that although Richard carried this practice to an extreme degree it was by no means so unusual as Pollard's valuable pioneering article would lead us to suppose.

J.E.A. Jolliffe pointed out, with a wealth of supporting evidence, that during the Angevin period, when England was more or less developing as a law state and the first foundations of the common law were established, acute tensions developed between the inert, conservative forces of local, feudal, and honorial traditions which feudal tenants and gentry regarded as a means of protecting their traditional rights and the arbitrary actions of kingship which were perhaps necessary if government was to operate at all effectively.[21] All three Angevin kings, Henry ii and Richard i hardly less than John, treating the country more or less as *dominium*, as royal demesne, expressed their power in outrageously arbitrary action against individuals though *vis et voluntas qui non sunt lex*,[22] imposing distraint and disseissin upon their tenants without judgment of any kind, let alone that *judicium baronum, judicium parium*, which clause 39 of Magna Carta later in reaction demanded. Royal *ira* and *malevolentia*, with assumed, unspoken licence to royal servants to oppress and harass the victims of such an exhibition of power, were enough in themselves to inflict a condition amounting to a disastrous state of unofficial outlawry upon even a powerful prelate or a secular magnate.[23] Such things were possible in the twelfth century when the restraining concept of the 'community of the realm' had hardly yet developed. However, as the concept of the community of the realm advanced as the thirteenth century advanced, the sentiments of the local communities expressed themselves more and more strongly in opposition to the arbitrary tendencies in the monarchy through the development first of baronial councils to guide, and even control, the king, and then of parliament.

This new combination once again produced its own deleterious side effects. The developing royal courts of justice, with their increasing masses of rules and their increasing formalism, provided the opportunity for almost equally illegitimate exploitations from the other side. In a highly contentious society, men more often regarded the law as a mass of technicalities to be exploited and litigation as a means of pursuing feuds than as vehicles of impartial justice – an attitude shared by kings themselves. Given such an outlook, as M.T. Clanchy has expressed it, 'It might even be argued that royal power contributed to disorder and corruption and that the judicial authority of the crown was a public nuisance.'[24] Certainly during the late thirteenth and the fourteenth centuries the royal justices enjoyed an appalling reputation for partiality, self-seeking, and corruption,[25] and by 1300 there was already a general feeling that disorder had reached crisis proportions[26] – a disillusionment with and a distrust of the law which found vehement expression both in parliament and in popular literature.[27]

During the fourteenth and fifteenth centuries the crown lost a good part of this arbitrary power both against its greater subjects and against the gentry of the shires. The control of great estates and the affinities which they supported was always a major factor in medieval politics, and with the amalgamation of great estates through the marriage of heiresses such aristocratic combinations grew more and more dangerous in the later Middle Ages. The Anglo-Norman kings had manipulated the tenure of the great fiefs almost at will. Only in the early twelfth century did the hereditary principle become firmly established.[28] Henry ii, Richard i, and John had dealt with the possessions of their tenants-in-chief in a thoroughly arbitrary manner.[29] Even at the end of the thirteenth century Edward i could manipulate magnate inheritances for the benefit of the crown without dangerous consequences.[30] Under Edward iii the balance between crown and nobility in the control of land tipped in favour of the nobility. In 1327 a new statute, in effect, gave tenants-in-chief the right to alienate holdings as they wished. Moreover, Edward iii showed no reluctance to grant licences for enfeoffments to uses, thus further lessening royal control.[31] When Edward iv, like Edward i, tried in the late 1470s to manipulate magnate inheritances to the advantage of his own family and to the detriment of collateral heirs at common law, his actions caused such resentment that the families who suffered supported Richard iii to the exclusion of Edward's heir.[32] It is true that Henry vii was able to break up the formidable and politically menacing Warwick inheritance without dangerous repercussions. This, however, was his only attempt at such direct action and circumstances were exceptionally favourable for the attempt.[33] On the other hand, his arbitrary manipulation of justice, to some extent reminiscent of the Angevin period, and his harsh control of the nobility through attainders, bonds, and recognizances, like his exploitation of the crown lands, was producing a dangerous backlash of resentment by 1509.[34]

Violent though life still was in the fifteenth century, and by modern standards it was appallingly violent, the upper ranks of landed society had gained at the expense of the monarchy. They were far better 'dug in' than they had been earlier in the control of their property and, therefore, of their local influence.

Again, royal control of the keeping of the peace and of justice, which had grown very prominently during the thirteenth century, weakened before local resistance compounded by financial inability to develop even an adequately centralized judicial bureaucracy. In consequence the crown waged, and lost, something like a running battle for local control with the more privileged inhabitants of the county communities – a defeat which, in the opinion of one authority, merely transferred the opportunities for violence and corruption to different hands.[35]

As England had developed a centralized government before it acquired a bureaucracy, a good deal of local administration had always to be carried out by local men of property.[36] Such people, accustomed from time immemorial to running their own affairs, had always resented the intrusion of the servants of the central government into their localities. During the twelfth century, in reaction against the magnate-curial sheriffs of the Anglo-Norman period – often corrupt and oppressive in the extreme like the notorious Picot of Cambridge – they had tried to insist on the appointment of local gentlemen to the shrivalties.[37] By the end of the second quarter of the thirteenth century the day of the curial sheriff was over.[38] By the end of the second quarter of the fourteenth century, however, even this was not enough for the local establishments. By the reign of Richard II the commons in parliament frequently petitioned not only for the appointment of resident gentlemen but, in addition, for annual replacements in office, thus limiting the effectiveness of the central government by preventing the development of an experienced corps of more or less permanent officials which would have increased the likelihood of what the commons regarded as excessive royal interference in the shires.[39] Though fifteenth-century kings did attempt to go back on such developments, the reaction was only partial and incomplete. Under Henry VI, and again to a more limited extent under Henry VII, officials of the royal household were appointed as sheriffs. In November 1436, for example, more than half the new sheriffs were household men. Even so, however, both kings seem to have kept to the letter of the law by seeing that such sheriffs were also local gentlemen. They came to hold office rather earlier in their careers than they might otherwise have done.[40]

A lack of trained personnel reinforced these prejudices. The thirteenth century had been an age of new judicial centralization articulated through the administrative-cum-judicial institution of the general eyre. By 1300, however, the eyre had broken down, totally overburdened by a vastly increased amount of royal business combined with a tremendous load placed upon it by the growing demands of the poorer classes of litigants, particularly in cases involving the newly developed concept of trespass. New and more flexible alternatives to the eyre had to be found to provide links between the centre and local adminstration if the already acute crisis in the courts and public order were not to reach even more horrendous proportions. The small group of royal professionals which had served the eyre had become completely inadequate to staff the growing scale of Angevin government.[41] The solution, whether the king and the small core of professional judges liked it or not, was to delegate more and more authority to the local gentry – to staff new forms of government by what may be regarded as atavistic means.

An age of considerable judicial experiment followed in which the ultimate solution was found, though not without considerable controversy, reluctance, and misgiving, in the promotion of local gentlemen, that is the same group of men who provided the sheriffs, to the status of judges. One experiment which reached its peak in the first two decades of the fourteenth century, and thereafter rapidly declined, was the issue of special individual commissions of oyer and terminer, largely staffed by local men. In the end, however, this particular type of remedy seems to have become more of an abuse than the conditions which it was intended to alleviate. The commissions, which, on the whole, served the interests of the middling strata of local society, were widely and notoriously employed to pursue malicious suits and to indulge in county feuding – so much so that the learned investigator of the system has concluded that they were a negative rather than a positive force on the problem of public order and that they very much increased the already high level of dislike for courts and judges.[42]

More general types of commission ultimately prevailed after considerable struggles between representatives of different points of view and different interests.[43] Sir Geoffrey le Scrope, the chief justice of the King's Bench, favoured the revival of the general eyre dominated by a centralized professional staff.[44] The magnates, or some of them, wished to see the appointment of aristocratic conservators of the peace in each county. The commons in parliament, who were, one may assume, no less self-interested, repeatedly petitioned for the transformation of keepers of the peace,[45] appointed from amongst the local gentry, that is from amongst their own ranks, into justices of the peace. This may indeed have been the first time that the commons had developed a conscious policy upon a major public issue and it was a policy which slowly gained ground against opposition in high places. Finally a statute of 1361 made them justices by authorizing them to try 'all manner of felonies and trespasses,' though in practice they had already exercised such powers for the previous eleven years.[46] This was a major and permanent capitulation by the central government.

Even then, however, the struggles were not over. The gentry, having obtained power, as in the case of the sheriffs earlier discussed, for a time pressed the matter much further, demanding more or less a monopoly of local judicial power. In 1384, and continuing for the next few years, the commons in parliament launched a sustained attack on the liveried retainers of the magnates, claiming that their lawlessness rendered justice ineffective and increased the country's disorders. As a corollary to this policy the commons also demanded that magnates should be completely excluded from the commissions of the peace. For a few months in 1389 Richard II supported the commons' demands. The government reduced the size of the county commissions from an average of 12.5 to between six and nine. The new commissions included two or three legal experts, who would have been occasional members when they visited the shires, and the rest were drawn from the ranks of 'the most able men in their shires,' that is exclusively from the knights and esquires. There was a clean sweep of the peerage from the commissions. The commons' combined campaign against liveries and in favour of their own judicial dominance of the shires was, however, short-lived. From the beginning it was hopelessly unrealistic in the social and political conditions of the day, dominated as they were by clientage and bastard feudalism, in other words the powerful networks of patronage dominated by the aristocracy. The justices of the peace could hardly enforce many of their decisions without the backing of the most powerful men in their localities. By the early 1390s the lords had once more returned to the commissions.[47]

The beginning of the Lancastrian period is generally said to have marked the success of the commons' policy of local self-government by the knights and esquires of the counties – or at least by the upper third of them who generally formed the commission of the peace – with only a very limited involvement by the crown.[48] Such opinions, however, call for some qualification. By 1439 complaints were heard that too many justices of too little property were being appointed, by whom the people would not be ruled and who, because of their comparative poverty, were guilty of extortion.[49] On the other hand, great magnates, with the weakening of royal control, were, through their influence on royal appointments,[50] and through their networks of clients who filled many local offices, able to dominate the affairs of some counties for long periods.[51] Although, of course, conditions varied immensely from region to region, even from shire to shire, lordship and local government were inextricably intertwined with varying results. At the same time the increasing size of the commissions during the fifteenth century[52] drew more and more of the gentry into the local circles of power. Further consolidation of local control might be inferred from this development. Any such inference may well, however, be mistaken. There are some indications that the monarchy began to fight back. Richard II, Henry VI, Edward IV, and Henry VII all tried for brief periods to dilute the local gentry in many areas with courtiers and officials, and Henry VII also placed a group of prominent, trusted ecclesiastics (some of whom he later promoted to bishoprics) on a large number of county commissions.[53] Moreover, all through the fifteenth century the central government continued to interfere in local affairs through the issue of numerous special commissions.[54]

Nevertheless, even when qualifications of this kind have been taken into account, property holding was the basic factor in local government, that is the major section of all government at the time. 'Government was a function of property,' only somewhat tempered by a limited degree of interference by the central government. In the social, economic, and fiscal conditions of the day it was largely conducted through clientage or bastard feudalism, whether or not we define bastard feudalism as restricted to certain categories of indentured retainers as defined by contemporary law on the subject, or as comprising those wider, somewhat ill-defined networks of relationship known as affinities. From 1885 (when the Oxford historian Charles Plummer invented the term 'bastard feudalism') until recently, historians have excoriated the phenomenon, distorting it by comparing its brutal facts with a highly idealized vision of earlier classical feudalism.[55] It is pointless to wax unduly moralistic about the defects of bastard feudalism, for there was no feasible alternative to it. English government from Anglo-Saxon times until the nineteenth century was based on property. Bastard feudalism was only one mutation of a basic system which endured for centuries[56] and it can be plausibly argued that it was more subtle, refined, and flexible and no more violent than classical feudalism had ever been, but obviously it still left the detailed exercise of local power in the hands of the local rich. Government was a co-operative effort between the monarchy and the aristocracy.

Repugnant though this may seem to us and to recent genera-tions of historians, contemporaries never attacked the system as such, only its fringe abuses. Indeed, as I have shown elsewhere, widespread opinion regarded government by the rich, by the well-established rich, as likely to be less corrupt than government by poorer men, in particular to be less corrupt than government by parvenus.[57] They were also completely realistic about the location of power. Sir John Fortescue, royal judge though he was, while admitting the tenure of a royal office added immensely to the holder's power and influence, nevertheless concluded that the power of the great lords of the land was greater than the power of the king's officers.[58]

The system functioned, one might say, both at the highest political level and in mundane day to day affairs. At the high political level the situation was exceedingly unstable, fluctuating almost from decade to decade. The immense, and immensely expensive, retinue of John of Gaunt[59] paid handsome dividends in helping to put his son, Henry IV, on the throne and to keep him there. A.L. Brown has very strongly pointed out how aristocratic aloofness so isolated Henry that it forced him to depend to an unusual extent upon a retinue of lesser property holders, of knights and esquires, with very unpleasant political side-effects. The need to reward the member of this retinue with land grants, pensions, and offices seriously depleted his finances (or so his suspicious subjects alleged), leading to demands for taxation to make up the deficits, which taxation made him very unpopular with the house of commons.[60] The unfortunate Henry IV badly needed the support of such a retinue, for aristocratic alienation from the monarchy reached one of its peaks in the early years of his reign. In 1403 when Henry Percy I, earl of Northumberland, had certainly been in arms against the king, the lords refused to convict him of treason or felony but only of trespass.[61] This was indeed a reversion to ruling *per judicium baronum* which, had it continued, would have made government quite impossible, as J.E.A. Jolliffe claimed for an earlier period.[62]

The lack both of a similar large retinue and of support from the peers proved a serious handicap to Richard of York in the 1450s.[63] Henry VI, in this troubled decade, in spite of his feebleness and wilfulness retained the support of the peerage for a surprisingly long time.[64] The failure of Henry VI and his council to arbitrate justly in the affairs of the nobility (one of the most important functions of royalty and one which was essential for the maintenance of good order in the countryside) not only led to the escalation of private feuds but resulted in the most serious inconveniences for many of the peerage. During the late 1440s and the 1450s at least one-sixth of the titled aristocracy were imprisoned for short periods for violent conduct.[65] Even so, thirty-two noble families fought for Henry before and during 1461. Again, between 1459 and 1461 four-fifths of the peerage were involved in battles. After that they became intensely suspicious and wary, disinclined to risk their lives and their estates for the sake of Edward IV at the end of his insecure and none too successful first reign. Nor would they take risks for an usurper of Richard III's notorious reputation by 1485 or put their money on an untried adventurer like Henry of Richmond. At

Bosworth Field, of the mere nine peers who are known to have ridden into battle with Richard six had profited financially from royal grants and concessions and only a little family party supported Henry vii.[66] By the end of the fifteenth century the aristocracy had become wary, cautious, and aloof at the highest level of politics.[67] As Sir Francis Bacon with considerable insight remarked, 'for his [Henry's] nobles, they were loyal and obedient, yet did not co-operate with him but let every man go his own way.'[68] Even so, Henry vii would probably have regarded this analysis as unduly rosy. As I have shown elsewhere, by the end of his reign four-fifths of the peerage were, or at some time had been, under the brutal penalties of suspended attainders or were bound *in terrorem* under ruinously heavy bonds and recognizances. They may well have heaved a huge collective sigh of relief at the news of Henry's death.[69]

At the everyday local level, government had, more or less, to be left to local people. Cities and boroughs controlled their own affairs, in theory subjecting the population to the most minute supervision: a supervision carried out by the citizens themselves, holding office in rotation, performing duties which in these days would be carried out by paid officials.[70] In the countryside most local cases were most probably still heard in the manorial courts.[71] Yet, on the whole, social discipline still lay in the hands of the aristocracy and gentry. In the last resort, for example, when lesser measures had failed, commissions of arrest were issued to peers.[72] Edward iv, in spite of intense personal activity in making judicial tours throughout the country,[73] found it advisable to increase the power of various nobles in their own localities, to create new spheres of interest for others and to endow them appropriately.[74] Conditions varied widely in different counties. Some, like Leicestershire with Lord Hastings under Edward iv and Lancashire then and later with the earls of Derby, were dominated by peers.[75] In Cheshire, on the other hand, about sixty gentry families, many of them related by marriage, between them controlled local affairs.[76] Much depended upon the personalities involved. East Anglia in mid-century suffered from the tyranny and violence of William, duke of Suffolk (died 1450) and John, duke of Norfolk (died 1461).[77] Richard, duke of Gloucester's 'lordship' in the north in the late seventies and the early eighties was probably over-lax and wasteful in order to gain popularity.[78] At the turn of the century the second Stanley earl of Derby (died 1521) was himself the greatest threat to public order in Lancashire.[79] On the other hand, the absence of a dominant great nobleman could lead to deplorable conditions. This was the case in Wales and the Marches where the great landlords were absentees. By the late fifteenth century the problem of disorder was due less to the existence of the Marcher lordships and the power of their lords than to the excessive feebleness of their government, losing power, both economic and administrative, to the turbulent, rising Welsh gentry – the inefficiency, oppression, and corruption of the gentry leading to the Act of Union of 1536, which, as Ralph Griffiths has remarked, was less an act of union with England than an act unifying the administration and the judicial system of Wales itself.[80]

At its best, people by no means resented aristocratic and gentry control. On the contrary they detested the corruption which ensued when poor men controlled or influenced affairs.[81] By the fifteenth century the common-law courts were so notoriously inefficient[82] that men took their quarrels for arbitration to the baronial councils of magnates.[83] Some did so because such methods were quicker: others no doubt somewhat unwillingly for fear of otherwise giving offence. In 1452 after Charles Nowell, one of the Mowbray affinity, had attacked John Paston in Norwich, Paston wrote:

And this notwithstanding, assone as knolech was had of my Lords coming to Framlingham, I never attemptid to procede ageyns hym as

justis and law wuld, but to trust to my seyd Lord that his Hyghnes wold
se this punischichid.[84]

Even so, magnates were not so dominant as magnates in other
countries of Europe. Unlike those of France, who controlled solid
blocs of territory, the estates of the great English aristocracy were
widely scattered, interspersed with those of others of equal
stature. Consequently their relations towards their gentry affinities were a peculiar functioning amalgam of dominance and
co-operation.[85] Even the Percies in the north, powerful as they
were, and although they spent a colossal proportion of their
resources on patronage as compared with other magnates,[86] were,
as a recent article has shown, severely restricted in their activities
by the opinions of their tenantry and their affinity.[87] 'Bad
lordship' could reduce a magnate to near impotence. Edward,
duke of Buckingham (died 1521) was so unpopular with his
Welsh and Marcher tenants that he needed an escort of three or
four hundred armed men to make a progress through his estates
and for that he had to obtain a licence from the crown.[88] The
countryside was ruled by self-help delicately poised upon a
balance of compromise, which differed from area to area, but
generally with a minimum of interference from the central
government.

3

Propaganda,
Compensations,
and the State of
the Country

FIFTEENTH-CENTURY ENGLISH KINGS commanded very little coercive or financial power. In the day-to-day affairs of government they were forced to rely upon the co-operation of the aristocracy and gentry, and that co-operation was given only within very constricting limits. It may well be that an acute realization of their practical weaknesses drove them to indulge in considerable propaganda efforts and in that propaganda to emphasize more and more strongly ideas of legitimacy and the theocratic nature of monarchy expressed in ritual and ceremony: a psychological compensation for diminished practical powers.

Some of these ceremonies were deliberate imitations of French practices. At their coronations the French kings were traditionally anointed with the sacred oil of Clovis, an oil of miraculous origin, which surrounded them with an especially sacred aura. An attempt to imitate this impressive form of sanctity arose in England, an attempt connected with political prophecies developing round the very popular cult of St Thomas of Canterbury. The origin of these prophecies cannot be dated before 1204 (thirty-four years after the saint's death) and they reached their complete form about 1340.

According to this prophetic literature, the Virgin Mary appeared in a vision to the saint in exile while he was praying in the church of St Colombe in Sens. There she presented Thomas with a golden eagle containing a stone ampoule filled with oil and instructed him that the oil was to be used in the coronations of future kings who would then in their great might recover Normandy and Anjou without the use of force. The oil had been 'discovered' by 1318, for then Edward II asked the advice of Pope John XXII about the feasibility of a reanointing. Although no evidence exists that Edward ever was reanointed, it seems plausible to interpret this correspondence with the pope as part of a plan to bolster up the position of an extremely unpopular king. The oil then disappeared, hidden in a church near Poitiers. According to Thomas of Walsingham, it was later rediscovered by a certain holy man who presented it to Edward III's son, the Black Prince. Once more the golden eagle and the ampoule disappeared, hidden in a locked chest in the Tower of London, to be rediscovered again in 1399. At this point Richard II demanded reanointing, but this was refused by Archbishop Arundel on the ground that such a sacrament, once administered, could not be repeated. The miraculous oil was, in fact, first used at the coronation of the Lancastrian usurper, Henry IV, thus adding a distinctly new aura to the ceremony.[1] Much good it may have done him, for according to one legend it produced a crop of lice in his hair, which people took for a bad omen.

Equally interesting were the innovations made at the coronation of Henry VI in 1429 and at the accession ceremonies of Edward IV in 1461. Some time before 1449 William Say, the dean of Henry's chapel, made for Count Alvaro Vaz d'Almada, who four years before had been made a Knight of the Garter, a copy of the *Liber regie capelle*, or Book of the Chapel Royal, for presentation to Alfonso V of Portugal.[2] This unique manuscript, now in the public library at Evora, shows that Henry VI's advisers, once again French-influenced, instituted significant changes in the coronation *ordo* directly adopted from the new redaction of the French coronation *ordo* made for Charles V of France in 1365.[3] These fifteenth-century changes reverted to, and most strongly stressed, the theocratic nature of kingship as against a more recent emphasis upon its limited or constitutional nature developed during the fourteenth century.

The first ceremony of the *ordo*, the ceremony of the *recognitio* by the people, was the last vestige of the ancient element of popular election in the monarchy. The French kings had completely ejected this ceremony from their coronation rite. Henry VI's presumably clerical advisers, whoever they were, did not dare to go to such extreme lengths, but they drastically downgraded the *recognitio* by relegating it from the first to the second stage of the proceedings, thus reducing its significance. As a result of this change the choir of the chapel royal was to chant the anthem *Ecce mitto angelum meum* and the bishop of Durham was to say the prayer *Omnipotens, sempiterne deus, qui famulum suum* before the king was ceremonially raised from his seat in Westminister Hall. Thus the clergy now greeted Henry as king *before* instead of after the *recognitio,* thus emphasizing the theocratic nature of the monarchy as against the popular element.[4] These changes, as Walter Ullman points out, introduce theocratic conceptions 'that all the earlier English coronation services ... have studiously avoided.'[5] Ullman considers that these ceremonial changes, together with the use of the miraculous oil, instead of oil merely bought from an apothecary's shop, were intended 'to strengthen an already rather battered theocratic function of the king in order to recoup his position vis-a-vis parliament.'[6] In addition, from about 1450 Henry vi was depicted in illuminated manuscripts wearing a closed imperial crown instead of an open royal crown.[7]

Edward iv's accession ceremonies were rather more contradictory in their nature, but once again the major emphasis was placed upon the theocratic elements. Edward, put upon the throne as he was in a crisis by a fragment of a faction,[8] was forced to bring every possible type of claim into play in order to bolster up his weak position. Throughout the earlier crisis of 1460, Edward's father, Richard, duke of York, had based his claim to the throne upon exclusively legitimist arguments.[9] As C.A.J. Armstrong has pointed out, however, to turn such a *de jure* title into *de facto* possession of the throne required some kind of public ceremony.[10] In the critical days of late February and early March 1461, no parliament was sitting and there was no time in which to summon one. A form of public recognition was, therefore, hastily improvised. On Sunday, 1 March, a crowd numbering possibly several thousand people assembled (or was organized) at St John's Fields, Clerkenwell. After an oration by George Neville, bishop of Exeter, the crowd acclaimed 'King Edward'[11] – surely a form of popular *recognitio.* Three days later, after a sermon

by George Neville at St Paul's Cross, another crowd again acclaimed Edward. Following this second acclamation Edward and
his retinue rode to Westminster Hall, where, before the archbishop of Canterbury, the chancellor, and various 'other lords,'
he swore an oath, which although its terms were somewhat
vague, more or less reproduced the substance of the coronation
oath. He then put on royal robes and a cap of estate – the cap of
estate being a symbol of majesty inferior in significance only to
the crown itself. After that he took his seat on the marble chair
in the court of the King's Bench – an enthronement which was a
symbolic mark of possession of the kingdom. He was then, once
again, proclaimed king.

Elaborate and impressive though these ceremonies were, there
was nothing particularly unusual about them. What followed,
however, was definitely startling. After this secular enthronement the procession returned to the abbey where Edward was
once again enthroned to the strains of a *te Deum*. Those present
then chanted before him *laudes regiae*, lauds of majesty:

Verus Vox, Rex Edwardus
Rectus Rex, Rex Edwardus
Justus, juridicus et legitimus Rex, Rex Edwardus
Cui ommnes hos subjici volumus
Suaeque humillima iuguns admittere subernationis.

This was nothing less than the ritual veneration of the quasi-
sanctified person of the enthroned ruler.

This impressive ceremony was a most significant liturgical
revival. The chanting of lauds of majesty before the enthroned
ruler had begun in the later Roman Empire. It had reached its
climax in England in the later thirteenth century when lauds had
been frequently sung before Henry III. Thereafter the practice
had declined. Lauds had been offered at Edward II's coronation.
They may possibly have been offered at Richard II's.[12] Then they

disappeared for nearly a century. Their revival in 1461 must have been an act of deliberately conscious antiquarianism – and, moreover, an act in what had now surely become a whole series of clerical efforts to exalt the theocratic nature of kingship.

Interesting as it was, however, probably only a small highly educated clerical public could understand the full significance of this sudden revival of lauds of majesty. In late medieval England, below the level of these extremely erudite clerics, there was (by the standards of the time) a large and cultivated public which welcomed reading matter.[13] Less learned efforts were needed to spread the appeal of monarchy to these wider, but less sophisticated, audiences. Such methods were employed both by the Yorkists and earlier by the Lancastrians – within limits. There was no counterpart in England to the contemporary Burgundian and French official histories and apologiae until such were commissioned by Henry vii from Polydore Vergil, the blind poet Bernard André, and John Skelton – and even then they were in Latin, so as to reach international as well as the more educated English audiences.[14] Other types of propaganda were, however, aimed at other types of people. The spread of literacy during the late fourteenth and fifteenth centuries and the emergence of a form of standard English based upon the language of the royal Signet Office and Chancery made it both possible and necessary to counteract the circulation of seditious rumours. Both governments and their opponents became increasingly aware of the importance of influencing the opinions of the political nation through the dissemination of handbills and pamphlets.[15] After the death of Henry v the government indulged in a very spate of propaganda to bolster up the fortunes of the new dual monarchy of England and France. J.W. McKenna has described the issue for the French territories of a new gold coin, the salute, which represented England as an angel announcing the coming of a saviour to France – a bizarre perversion of the annunciation scene, exceptionally daring as the cult of Blessed Virgin was one of the most popular forms of devotion at this time. Even the pastries and the jellies at court banquets were made into shapes symbolic of the dual monarchy. The duke of Bedford commissioned from the French poet Lawrence Callot a poem stressing the king's dual English and French descent – a poem which, together with a pictorial genealogy, was posted on the walls of major churches across northern France, thus taking advantage both of visual impact and of growing literacy amongst the population. In 1426 the earl of Warwick ordered the famous Bury St Edmund's monk, John Lydgate, to translate Callot's poem into English. Enormous numbers of copies must have been reproduced, for no less than forty-six still survive, many of which show signs of being posted as bills or possibly even as school texts to be learned by heart.[16] John Gower also wrote propaganda poems, and government-sponsored pageants by Lydgate were apparently highly successful. Humphrey of Gloucester commissioned the Italian humanist Tito Livio da Forli to write a panegyric of his brother Henry v, and, with typical conceit, another of himself, *The Humphrodiad*, both again in Latin.[17] John Fortescue's pamphlets in favour of the Lancastrian succession, couched though they were in lawyer's Latin, were powerful enough (their appeal must have been to the provincial gentry, the powerful affinities of the great lords and their like) for the Yorkist government to demand refutations before taking him into favour.[18]

Another development under Edward IV and Henry VII was the development of widely publicized heralds' reports in English and the circulation of official newsletters like the *Arrivall* of 1471, immediately sent abroad to justify Edward IV's invasion of England, and the *Spousells of the Princess Mary* of 1508, translated into French for their effects on the continent abroad.[19]

Another type of Yorkist propaganda also appealed to wider audiences than the revived liturgical ceremonial, though still to comparatively small lay sections – the nobility, the gentry, and the more educated of the merchant class. This is shown by a group of comparatively luxurious manuscripts, intended for leisured perusal – the production of which in considerable number may have been consciously planned. They contain genealogies largely based upon the twelfth-century Geoffrey of Monmouth's *Historia Regum Britanniae*, stressing Edward iv's descent from biblical times.[20] Moreover, writings in that very popular genre, political prophecy, attributed the kingdom's troubles to divine retribution on the country's wickedness in tolerating the Lancastrian usurpation[21] – a theme which had been elaborated in a propaganda speech during the 1461 inauguration ceremonies and which had been reproduced more or less verbatim in parliament later in the year.[22] In the same parliament the speaker, Sir James Strangeways, a connection of the Nevilles, the new king's closest allies, had delivered an oration in almost religious phraseology on Edward's title and his royal attributes.[23] Finally, Richard iii made a strong appeal to the legitimist principle when he justified his usurpation on the ground that, owing to the bastardy of his brother and his nephews, he alone represented the pure, uncorrupted, ancient blood royal.[24]

Kings supported theories with increasing visual splendour. The later Middle Ages were a period of the growth of courts in which royal establishments became far larger and more magnificent than the baronial households which they had formerly resembled.[25] Although the Black Book of the Household of 1478 was compiled to introduce economies into the royal household, its author wrote that kings ought to be magnificent 'which means superabundant liberality' ('super habundans liberalitas').[26] Royal magnificence was a most effective manifestation of political propaganda and authority: Henry v's helmet at Agincourt was plated with pure gold and encircled by a crown studded with sapphires and rubies and one hundred and twenty-eight pearls.[27] By the fifteenth century ceremonial crown-wearings had become considerably more frequent than they had been earlier – to the earlier crown-wearing ceremonies of Christmas, Easter, and

Whitsuntide were added those of Epiphany, All Saints, and the two feasts of Edward the Confessor. Also new was the institution of a crown-wearing ceremony for the queen on the anniversary of her coronation.[28] The queen's churching was also conducted with great formality, requiring the assistance of two dukes in helping her out of bed.[29]

Although in 1471 a London mob derided Henry VI for his shabby appearance,[30] during his reign more than one foreign observer had been impressed by the splendours of the Lancastrian court.[31] Henry himself had gone richly dressed. Margaret of Anjou had been escorted to England for her marriage with almost unparalleled pomp, and the London pageants arranged for her coronation, sponsored by the king himself, were the occasion of 'a gigantic display of propaganda' for the dynasty and the government's current peace policies.[32] Later the courts of Edward IV and Henry VII became equally, if not more, impressive. Edward IV became a definite trend-setter in male fashions.[33] Even in the impecunious days of his return from exile in 1471 he spent very considerable sums of money on new clothes,[34] a striking contrast to Henry VI at the same time. In 1465 the Bohemian nobleman, Leo of Rozmital, was impressed by the extremely formal ceremonial of the court. On the evening after her churching after the birth of one of her children the queen sat alone at table on a costly golden chair, and after a dinner lasting three hours, during which not a word was spoken, dancing began. During the dance the queen's mother, the duchess of Bedford, knelt before her all the time except when at intervals she was bidden to rise.[35] A similar type of deference had earlier been paid to Margaret of Anjou.[36] Festivities, tournaments, and the entertainment of foreign magnates were costly and splendid.[37] The ducal court of Burgundy, at that time the most lavishly splendid in Europe, became the great example for the Yorkists. Edward's queen, Elizabeth Wydeville, and her family had close connections with this court[38] and it had strongly impressed the king himself during his brief exile from 1470 to 1471. Then in 1475 he asked Olivier de la Marche for a written description of the state kept by the Duke Charles the Bold in his household and on the battlefield to serve as a model for new household ordinances of his own.[39]

Henry VII was no less anxious to make the maximum impression both upon his own subjects and upon foreigners. Avaricious as he was in the accumulation of money, he was far from miserly in spending it[40] and spared no expense in ostentatious ceremonial and building. He always went extremely richly dressed and wore costly jewels.[41] Amongst other things he instituted the elaborate and expensive collar which is still part of the insignia of the Order of the Garter. Nor did he stint money in building his chapel at Westminister to rival St George's, Windsor, which had almost certainly been erected as a cult centre to glorify the Yorkist dynasty. As several writers have pointed out, the architectural forms of the Westminister chapel express an extremely elaborate royalist symbolism, going in its origins as far back as Boethius. Much the same symbolism was also employed in magnificent pageants, one of which even went so far as symbolically to identify Prince Arthur with God the Son and the king himself with God the Father.[42]

The Wydevilles were still very prominent indeed at the early Tudor court. Not only was Henry's queen the daughter of Elizabeth Wydeville but her cousin, Sir Edward, had joined Henry of Richmond in exile and had been rewarded with the Order of the Garter. Both Edward Stafford, third duke of Buckingham, and Henry Bouchier, second earl of Essex, were the queen's nephews, and her aunt, Catherine Wydeville, the dowager duchess of Buckingham, had married the king's uncle, Jasper, duke of Bedford. The future earls of Surrey and Devon were married to sisters of the queen and the marquesses of Dorset were descendants of Elizabeth Wydeville by her first marriage to Sir John Grey of Groby. The influence of the Low Countries remained strong. In fact it became more predominant than ever before, making Edward IV's earlier cultural borrowings look distinctly amateurish.[43] Henry VII completely accepted the Burgundian theme of Magnificence as one of the principal attributes of monarchy, so much so that after a disastrous fire at Sheen on 30 December 1497 he spent £15,000 on building Richmond Palace in the very latest Flemish and northern French style – brick-built with many towers and enormous windows. A modern writer has described it as 'a palace where great events of the reign could have fitting setting.'[44] Popularly known from its splendour as England's 'Rich Mount,' even Burgundians admired it, and it was notably conspicuous in days when monastic rather than royal and aristocratic buildings were still the grandest edifices in the English countryside.[45] The Great Hall of Richmond emphasized the propaganda theme with, between its high windows, a series of portraits (probably painted by the Walloon artist Maynard) of those English kings notable for the military virtues – Brute, Arthur, Richard the Lionheart, and Edward III amongst others, executed in the new three-quarter bust portrait style developed by Rogier van der Weyden – all leading up to the triumph of Henry VII, whose own portrait was placed at the end of the hall. Again, if Edward IV's public spectacles had been gorgeous, they were far exceeded by the preparations made for the reception of Catherine of Aragon. Here, significantly enough, there were jousts which transformed the rather old-fashioned English style of tournament, which had been predominantly a martial exercise, into an allegorical propaganda pageant copied from well-established Burgundian models. By the end of the fifteenth century the English court had probably become one of the most splendid and formal in Europe and the most prominent centre for propaganda for the royal dynasty.

To sum up, what can we say of the monarchy and of the state of the country at the end of the fifteenth century? There is very little in late-fourteenth and fifteenth-century English writing to justify the title of political thought: just a collection of time-hallowed clichés and prejudices, which, however, were held very strongly indeed. These traditional views limited the pretensions of monarchy at almost every turn. Fourteenth-century constitutional developments had severely restricted legal activities and a hardening of legal attitudes had severely reduced arbitrary action against individuals of the type which Anglo-Norman monarchs and the Angevin kings of the twelfth century had freely indulged in. Unlike their French counterparts, English kings could neither legislate nor tax in virtue of their own unfettered will. They could legislate and tax only in parliament and they were themselves under the law and not above it. Even so, probably the dominance of the common law rather than parliament was the main defence of English liberties, for from 1461 parliament was meeting less and less frequently.[46] During the last twelve years of his reign Henry VII summoned only one parliament. In practice, contemporary conventions confined the role of government to defence and 'justice.' The overwhelming sanctity of property severely restricted the scope of monarchical power. Even foreign policy centred on the concept of inheritance. Even so, from the time of Henry V's death, if not before, the willingness of the political nation to bear the cost of prosecuting the king's rights in France by warlike means seriously diminished. Moreover, as England was an island, the need for defence was less apparent, less urgent, than in continental states with their extended and vulnerable land frontiers. Appeals for taxation for such purposes, therefore, fell upon deaf ears, so much so that after the final expulsion of the English from France in 1453 the commons in particular saw to it that English kings just could not finance an ambitious foreign policy. In foreign affairs their subjects had more or less castrated them. Even worse, by Henry VII's time even taxation imposed for defence generated ominous political tensions. Nor could kings demand taxation to meet the costs of domestic government, of 'justice.' Most of the functions of 'justice' were performed by the local men of property, who, having successfully prevented the growth of local royal bureaucracies, were merely supervised and checked by the central authority both through the courts and through the distribution of patronage, a combination of rather primitive, limited bureaucracy and bastard feudalism. Even this supervision did no more than keep their activities within decent bounds, restricting the worst excesses of their self-interest and often not even that.

People complained endlessly in parliament and out of parliament of 'lack of governance,' to use the contemporary phrase. Yet in spite of their persistent wailings they were not really prepared to contemplate any extension of the central government's supervisory powers which might threaten the freedom of action of the local establishments. One of the most notable aspects of Henry vii's legislation against disorder was the temporary nature of a good deal of it.[47] Chief Justice Finieux (1488?–1527) commented on the apparent lack of will of both Henry vii and the magnates for the better enforcement of order,[48] and during Henry's reign prosecutions under penal statutes were far less extensive than they became later in the sixteenth century.[49] Local forces had perhaps become so dominant as to produce something like stalemate in government.

Possibly to counteract these limitations and weaknesses, the monarchs themselves placed increased emphasis upon the principle of legitimacy. Erudite ecclesiastical advisers and liturgiologists revived and borrowed foreign, particularly French, ideas of theocratic kingship. These, however, had the disadvantage of restricted appeal, being fully comprehensible only to a learned clerical audience, and could have compensated only in a very feeble way for the constitutional and practical limitations which historical developments and the social structure imposed on the English monarchy. More secular types of propaganda expressed in chronicles, in parliament, and in growing courtly magnificence may well have been more effective.

No one, nowadays, could accept the verdict on the 'New Monarchy' current for three generations or so after J.R. Green first invented the term[50] – that is, the Yorkists and Henry VII introduced a kind of incipient despotism based upon middle-class support, strong finances, the decline of parliament, and the ruin of a turbulent aristocracy already demoralized by the Wars of the Roses. Edward IV and Henry VII, in fact, rescued the country from its mid-century turmoils, which had been largely due to weakness of Henry VI and his inability to arbitrate fairly between the rivalries and the quarrels of the aristocracy. Even so, both of them and Richard III, all three, died with an unenviable reputation for tyranny: Edward for avarice and the unscrupulous manipulation of noble inheritances for the benefit of the royal family at the expense of the heirs-at-law,[51] Richard for usurpation, for the intrusion of hated northerners into local, southern power structures,[52] and for suspected murder,[53] Henry VII once more for avarice and for his terrorization of the nobility and other groups of his subjects.[54] Yet, even so, neither Edward nor Henry had ever dared to make a frontal attack upon the reform of the country's institutions as such. They worked on the margins in temporarily effective but politically irritating ways.

Though complaints seem to have died down by the end of the fifteenth century, by modern standards both personal conduct and public order were very low indeed. In the absence of a police force all free citizens were expected to assist in keeping the peace and all free men between the ages of sixteen and sixty were expected to possess and practise the use of arms. This in itself was exceedingly dangerous, and it was all the more dangerous when combined with lack of emotional restraint in the men of the day. Restraint of the emotions is a much more recent development than most people realize. Even in the mid-Victorian house of commons, both Gladstone and Disraeli were capable of shedding bucketsful of tears, and it is said that Gladstone was once so overcome by his own oratory that he burst into tears in the middle of one of his own speeches. In the late Middle Ages violent behaviour which today we generally associate only with hooligans and criminal types was appallingly common at all levels of society. The town of Oxford on the eve of the Black Death was a small place, with a population of probably about 5,500 plus 1,500 academics. Riots between town and gown and fights between northern and southern students were so common that Hastings Rashdall wrote, of the stretch of the High Street between St Martin's church and St Mary's church, 'There are historic battlefields on which less [blood] has been spilt.'[55] A recent study shows the homicide rate to have been between four and six times higher than those of modern Detroit, Atlanta, and New Orleans, three of the most violent cities of the modern United States.[56]

Again, take the following letters. On 23 August 1461 John Paston the eldest wrote to his father:

It is talkyd here how that ye and Howard schuld a' streyn togueder on the scher day, and that on of Howards men schuld a'strekyn you twyess with a dagere, and soo ye schuld a ben hurt but for a good dobelet that ye hadde on at that tyme.

The feud continued, for about seven weeks later Clement Paston wrote to John, when telling him to hurry to court in order to avoid Edward IV's displeasure,

Also it ye doe well, come right stronge, for Howards wife made her bost that if any of her husbands men might come to yow ther yulde goe no penny for your life.[57]

Now the Pastons and the Howards did not come from the dregs of society. They were rich East Anglian landowners, high in the social scale. In 1470 Sir John Howard received a barony and in 1483 as the collateral heir of the Mowbray family he inherited the dukedom of Norfolk, and a descendant of the Pastons in 1673 was created viscount and in 1679 earl of Yarmouth. Given such behaviour even on the part of the upper classes of the political nation, in the end the achievement of the monarchy can be considered no more than fragile.[58] As I have written elsewhere, to quote the words of one of Edward IV's signet letters, the most these insecure monarchs probably hoped for was that the country would 'sit still and be quiet.'[59] R.L. Storey wrote of the fifteenth century that even in the best-ordered of reigns the forces of authority were barely adequate 'and the internal peace of the kingdom was poised on a razor's edge.'[60] G.R. Elton's conclusions about the England of the 1530s are remarkably similar.[61] Governmental power was limited, restricted, and precarious. Therefore kings and their ministers had to move with wary caution in face of the shire establishments and their resentment against central interference in what they regarded as their own spheres of influence, particularly when a shire community itself was somewhat unstable and the government attempted to introduce new court-centred interests into the charmed circle of the older local families.[62] It is surely little wonder that for the purposes of propaganda they pressed into service every possible manifestation of literature, ceremonial and visual and artistic splendour.

Notes

CHAPTER ONE

1 P. de Commynes, *Mémoires*, ed. J. Calmette and G. Durville, 3 vols. (Paris 1924–5), 2: 207–37.
2 E.g., amongst many other examples, ibid., 1:24, 27, 38, 54, 109, 121, 182, 189, 233; 2:9, 28, 262.
3 Sir J. Fortescue, *De laudibus legum anglie*, ed. S.B. Chrimes (Cambridge 1942), especially chapters 12, 13, and 14.
4 He argued that *dominium politicum et regale* developed later than *dominium regale* 'whan mankynde was more mansuete, and bettir disposid to vertue.' Sir J. Fortescue, *The Governance of England*, ed. C. Plummer (Oxford 1885), 111–12. He argued that the Hundred Years' War had made it impossible for the French Estates General to meet; therefore kings began to tax arbitrarily and went on doing so so regularly that peasants' taxes had become five times greater than their rents. This crushing taxation, he went on, had reduced the French peasantry to such poverty that they could no longer serve as soldiers to defend the land, and he feared that arbitrary royal taxation, if it developed, would reduce the English to the same deplorable state. He thought that peasant prosperity resulted in better public order. Ibid., 114–18, 137–42. He also argued that it was dishonourable for a king to impoverish his people. For French conditions see also Fortescue, *De laudibus*, chapter 35, *Governance*, 139. Fortescue's description of the degradation of the French peasantry

was not the prejudiced vision of a homesick émigré. See below p. 3 and n. 5.

5 *Journal des États Généraux de France tenus à Tours en 1484,* ed. J. Masselin and A. Bernier, Collections de Documents Inedits sur l'Histoire de France (Paris 1835), 672–5.

6 J. Rous, *Historia regum anglie,* ed. J. Hearne (Oxford 1745), quoted in M. Beresford, *The Lost Villages of England* (London 1954), 81.

7 J.E. Thorold Rogers, *Six Centuries of Work and Wages: The History of English Labour* (London 1949), 233–42; E.H. Phelps-Brown and S.A. Hopkins, 'Seven Centuries of the Prices of Consumables, Compared with Builders' Wage Rates,' in *Essays in Economic History,* ed. E.M. Carus-Wilson, 2 (1962), 179–96.

8 Fortescue, *Governance,* 116; that is 1 Samuel 8:20, according to the modern arrangement of the Old Testament.

9 Fortescue, *Governance,* 116. In the same passage he continued his diatribe against the French monarchy, 'wich the French Kynge dothe not, though he kepe Justice be twene subiet and subiet: sithin he oppressith thaim more hym self, than wolde haue done all the wronge doers of the reaume, though thai had no kynge.'

10 E. Hall, *The Union of the Two Noble and Illustre Families of Lancastre and Yorke, commonly known as Hall's Chronicle* (London 1809), 67. For similar sentiments see *The Prologues and Epilogues of William Caxton,* ed. W.J.B. Crotch (Early English Text Society 1928), 12–16, 81.

11 In 1671 the duke of Albemarle (the ex-revolutionary General Monke) genially wrote: 'It is a great mistake to confuse the commons with the common people in England. The poorer and meaner people have no interest in the commonwealth but the use of breath.' Such views seem to have been commonplace enough at the time. Oliver Cromwell himself used very similar phrases. C. Hill, *The Century of Revolution* (London 1961), 310. At the end of the century, John Locke could state quite confidently: 'The great and chief end, therefore, of men's uniting into commonwealths and putting themselves under government, is the preservation of their property.' *The Second Treatise of Government,* ed. T.P. Peardon (New York 1953), 71.

12 H.M. Cam, 'Stubbs Seventy Years After,' *Cambridge Historical Journal,* 9 (1948), 144.

13 See S.B. Chrimes, *English Constitutional Ideas in the Fifteenth Century*

(Cambridge 1936), 9ff. J.R. Lander, 'Attainder and Forfeiture, 1453–1509,' *Historical Journal*, 9 (1961), 145–6 and nn. 104 and 105, reprinted in Lander, *Crown and Nobility, 1450–1509* (London and Montreal 1976), 155–6 and 155, nn. 104 and 105.

14 See the arguments put forward by Tito Livio da Forli on Henry v's claim to France. *The First English Life of Henry VI*, ed. C.L. Kingsford (Oxford 1911), 23ff.

15 See below pp. 32ff.

16 As early as 1318, the council declared that it required great deliberation in parliament to change the law. M. Prestwich, *The Three Edwards: War and State in England, 1272 to 1377* (London 1980), 126. In 1348 the king gave the following answer to a common petition: 'Autre foi le Roi, per avis des Prelatz et Grantz de la terre, Que eis eues et usees en temps passez, ne le Proces d'icelle usez cea en arere, ne se pourront changer saunz ent faire novel Estatut.' *Rot. Parl.*, ii, 203. See also T.F.T. Plucknett, *Statutes and Their Interpretation in the First Half of the Fourteenth Century* (Cambridge 1922), 126 and n. 2, app. 192; C.H. Putnam, *The Place in Legal History of Sir William Shareshull* (Cambridge 1950), 106; M. McKisack, *The Fourteenth Century, 1307–1399* (Oxford 1959), 195; B. Wilkinson, *The Later Middle Ages in England* (London 1969), 379; Fortescue, *De laudibus*, chapter 17. H.M. Cam, *Law-Finders and Law-Makers* (London 1962), 135; *Rot. Parl.*, ii, 203, 311, 368.

17 See below chapter 3, n. 6.

18 Roger of Hoveden, *Chronica*, ed. W. Stubbs, Rolls Series, 4 vols. (1868–71) 4:62–6. See also C.R. Young, *The Royal Forests of England* (Leicester 1979), 29.

19 J.R. Maddicott, *The English Peasantry and the Demands of the Crown, 1294–1341*, Past and Present Supplement 1 (1975), 14.

20 Sir G. Edwards, *The Second Century of the English Parliament* (Oxford 1979), lectures 2 and 3.

21 G.L. Harriss, *King, Parliament and Public Finance in Medieval England to 1369* (Oxford 1975), 370ff; 512–13; 'War and the Emergence of the English Parliament, 1297–1360,' *Journal of Medieval History*, 2 (1976), 35–56.

22 Prestwich, *The Three Edwards*, 68, 191–2.

23 In 1334 the fifteenth and tenth was standardized at £38,170.

McKisack, *The Fourteenth Century, 1307–1399*, 192. By contrast, in 1290 a fifteenth had brought in £117,000. M. Powicke, *The Thirteenth Century* (Oxford 1953), 524.

24 A.R. Bridbury, *Economic Growth: England in the Later Middle Ages* (London 1962), 96–7. In 1433 the tax was cut by 10.4 per cent, ostensibly to relieve decayed places no longer capable of paying (*Rot. Parl.*, iv, 425–6), but in fact every country got an equal remission of its quota as though all were equally poor. In 1446 the cut was increased to 15 per cent.

25 See Lander, *Crown and Nobility, 1450–1509*, 39–40 and 40 n. 214. For general resistance to taxation see *English Historical Documents*, vol. 4, 1327–1485, ed. A.R. Myers (London 1969), 379–81.

26 *A Relation, or Rather a True Account of the Island of England*, ed. C.A. Sneyd (Camden Ser. 1847), 52.

27 J.L. Bolton, *The Medieval English Economy, 1150–1500* (London and Totowa, NJ 1980), 297.

28 For detailed references see Lander, *Crown and Nobility, 1450–1509*, 43, nn. 230–3. In addition, the judges were well aware of the extreme reluctance of juries to bring in verdicts of guilty against defendants in customs prosecutions. C.G. Bayne and W.H. Dunham, Jr, *Select Cases in the Council of Henry VII* (Selden Society 1958), cxv.

29 J.R. Lander, *Government and Community: England 1450–1509* (London and Cambridge, Mass. 1980), 90–6.

30 H.G. Cobb, 'Books of Rates and the London Customs,' *Guildhall Miscellany*, 6:4 (1971), 1–12. Also, for the fictitious nature of the aulnage accounts during much of the century, see E.M. Carus-Wilson, 'The Aulnage Accounts: A Criticism,' *Economic History Review*, 2 (1929), 114–23.

31 B.P. Wolffe, *The Royal Demesne in English History: The Crown Estate in the Governance of the Realm from the Conquest to 1509* (London 1971), 40 and n. 90.

32 *Chronicon Adae de Usk, A.D., 1377–1421*, ed. Sir E. Maunde Thompson (London 1904), 8, 148–9.

33 Ibid., 133, 319–20. The extant Chronicle ends with this diatribe, the remainder being lost.

34 R.A. Griffiths, *The Reign of King Henry VI: The Exercise of Royal*

Authority, 1422–1461 (Berkeley 1981), 118. Even so it was more productive than similar expedients in 1428 and 1431.

35 It should be remembered that this tax was exceptional and that the peers did not contribute to the standard fifteenth and tenth. Sir J.H. Ramsay, *Lancaster and York*, 2 vols. (Oxford 1892) 1:109; A. Steel, *The Receipt of the Exchequer, 1377–1485* (Cambridge 1954), 273.

36 For a detailed account see J.R. Lander, 'The Hundred Years' War and Edward IV's 1475 Campaign in France,' in *Tudor Men and Institutions: Studies in English Law and Government*, ed. A.J. Slavin (Baton Rouge 1972), 84–9, reprinted in Lander, *Crown and Nobility, 1450–1509*, 228–34.

37 S.B. Chrimes, *Henry VII* (London 1972), 80 n. 1 and 199 n. 2.

38 J.H. Wylie, *History of England under Henry the Fourth*, 4 vols. (London 1884–98), 3:119.

39 The French war of 1512–14 was financed in part by the 'treasure' which Henry VII had left to his son and in part by loans. Taxation provided only about one-third of the money needed. Wolsey's lack of success in wringing money out of parliament and country in the 1520s is notorious. In spite of highly significant reforms in the system of direct taxation between 1513 and 1516, it was not until the late 1530s and the 1540s that the government successfully raised really large amounts of money from it. P. Williams, *The Tudor Regime* (Oxford 1979), 59–61; S.E. Lehmberg, *The Later Parliaments of Henry VIII, 1536–1547* (Cambridge 1977), chapter 5.

40 See J.R. Lander, *Government and Community: England, 1450–1509* (London and Cambridge, Mass. 1980). 285–92, 301–5. For more critical views of Yorkist and early Tudor foreign policy see C. Ross, *Edward IV* (London 1974), chapter 9.

41 B.P. Wolffe, *The Crown Lands, 1461–1536* (London and New York 1970), 1–28, and *The Royal Demesne in English History: The Crown Estate in the Governance of the Realm from the Conquest to 1509* (London 1971), chapters 1–3, 6–7. Chapters 6 and 7 of this latter book are revised versions of articles published in the *English Historical Review*, 71 (1956), 1–27 and 79 (1964), 225–54. Both versions need to be used, however, as the earlier versions contain materials not included in the revisions and vice-versa. J.J.N. Palmer, 'The Parliament of 1385 and the Constitutional Crisis of 1386,' *Speculum*, 46 (1973), 78.

Edward I had then declared 'que vous ne entendez a ceste foiz nule aide de nous demaunder ne autre foiz si graunt desoign ne le face, mes del votre demeyne chevir vous en ceste guerre taunt come vous purrez ... ' *Registrum Roberti Winchelsey*, ed. R. Graham, 2 vols. (Canterbury and York Society 1952–4), 1:260.

42 Fortescue, *De laudibus*, chapter 35; *Governance*, 113–15.

43 E.H. Kantorowicz, 'Inalienability,' *Speculum*, 29 (1954), 488–502, reprinted in E.H. Kantorowicz, *Selected Studies*, ed. M. Cherniavasky and R.E. Giesy (New York 1965), 138–50. Limitation on the king's power to alienate appears in one of the versions of the coronation oath. W. Stubbs, *The Constitutional History of England*, 3 vols. (Oxford 1870–8), 2: 105. Opposition to alienation may have grown considerably stronger in the fifteenth century. Henry IV's first parliament passed an act that all men who petitioned the king for grants should state the exact value of the grants asked for and also the value of any previous grants which they had received, though these restrictions were somewhat relaxed in the next parliament. *Rot. Parl.*, iii, 433, 458, *Statute Roll*, 2 Henry IV, c. 2. In 1404 the commons demanded that in future any officer who executed any grant out of the ancient inheritance of the crown should lose his office, forfeit everything he could forfeit to the crown, and be imprisoned for three years, and that anyone who accepted such a grant should lose it and be imprisoned for three years. *Rot. Parl.*, iii, 548. In 1443 when the duke of Somerset (whose main endowment lay in Exchequer annuities) asked for 1,000 marks' worth of land, the lords of the council 'durst not avise the kyng to depart from such livelode, ne to opon their mouthes in such matters.' Sir N.H. Nicolas, *Proceedings and Ordinances of the Privy Council*, 7 vols. (London 1834–7), 5: 253. In the end Henry VI granted 600 marks' worth of land. Fortescue (*Governance*, 134) trenchantly stated that a king might not 'honestly' sell his lands like other men, for that was delapidation, and quoted the notorious case of the sale of the Chirk Woods and the Chirk Lands. For details of this case see Fortescue, *Governance*, 274–5. In his will Edward IV exhorted his son Edward and his heirs not to alienate certain possessions from the crown 'as he and thay wil answere afore God at the day of Dome, and as they love the wele of thaim silf and of the said Reame.' J. Bentley, *Excerpta historica* (London 1833), 377.

44 Fortescue, *Governance*, 154–5.
45 See Lander, *Government and Community: England 1450–1509*, 103–4.
 Nor, in spite of considerable efforts, was the exploitation of the crown
 estates entirely successful. For the system's distinctly spotty record,
 see C.D. Ross, 'The Reign of Edward IV,' in *Fifteenth Century England,
 1399–1509: Studies in Politics and Society*, ed. S.B. Chrimes, C.D. Ross,
 and R.A. Griffiths (Manchester and New York 1972), 58–60; C. Ross,
 Edward IV (London 1974), 382–4; R. Somerville, *History of the Duchy of
 Lancaster*, 2 vols. (London 1953–70), 1, chapter 12, Public Record
 Office, DL 42/19. 103v, February 1482; E.M. Carus-Wilson, 'Evidences
 of Industrial Growth on Some Fifteenth Century Manors,' *Economic
 History Review*, 2nd ser., 2 (1959–60), 196–7.
46 The garrison of Calais was 1,120 in war, reduced to about 750 in
 peace-time, so in fact garrisons would drain off even more of the
 limited manpower available during periods of hostilities. *Calendar of
 Close Rolls, 1485–1500*, no. 1193. In 1508 the garrison of Berwick was
 to consist of 100 spears, 50 foot archers, 50 other foot soldiers, and 20
 gunners. In addition the castle was to have 32 soldiers plus officers
 and functionaries. If the Scots laid siege or invaded England there
 were to be another 400 soldiers. In 1488 the marshal of Berwick was to
 have another 24 soldiers. *Calendar of Close Rolls, 1500–1509*, no. 958,
 Public Record Office, E. 351/225. I owe these references to J.D. Alsop.
 I have not been able to ascertain the regular forces at Carlisle.
47 For Edward's guard, *Letters and Papers Illustrative of the Wars of the
 English in France*, ed. J. Stevenson, 2 vols in 3 (Rolls Series 1861–4), 2,
 pt. 2, 788.
48 Henry VII's yeomen numbered about fifty during the early years of
 the reign. J.D. Mackie, *The Early Tudors, 1485 to 1588* (Oxford 1952),
 58: but c. 1487 the Venetian envoy estimated them at three or four
 times this number. *A Relation, or Rather a True Account of the Island of
 England*, 39, 47.
49 *Calendar of State Papers and Manuscripts Existing in the Archives and
 Collections of Milan*, vol 1, ed. A.B. Hinds (London 1912), 322. By this
 time, English fortifications were completely out of date by continental
 standards, and many royal castles were in a ruinous condition. B.H.
 St J. O'Neil, *Castles and Cannon* (Oxford 1960), chapters 1–3. See also
 William Worcestre, *Itineraries*, ed. J.H. Harvey (Oxford 1969), 21, 23,

141. The same statement also applies to many magnate castles. By 1500, of the Welsh castles of the Stafford dukes of Buckingham, Brecon was partly ruinous, though it was then renovated and became Duke Edward's principal Welsh residence, but Newport was in a bad state and Hay, Huntingdon, Caurs, and Bronllys were beyond repair. It is clear that the Staffords were reluctant to spend money on buildings which they no longer needed as fortresses. T.B. Pugh, *The Marcher Lordships of South Wales, 1415 to 1536* (Cardiff 1963), 247. For general observations on the subject, see also J. Gillingham, *The Wars of the Roses: Peace and Conflict in Fifteenth-Century England* (London 1981), 15–44.

50 J.R. Hooker, 'Notes on the Organization and Supply of the Tudor Military' *Huntingdon Library Quarterly*, 23 (1959–60), 231–3.

51 *Edward IV's French Expedition of 1475: The Leaders and the Badges, being MS. 2 M16. College of Arms*, ed. F.B. Barnard (Oxford 1925) 1r–3v. Although feudal tenures were obsolete from the military point of view, magnates and the greater gentry expected their tenants and servants to serve them in war at their own expense. In 1482 Edward Mauleverer, a Yorkshire squire, made it incumbent on his tenants to be well armed at their own expense and prepared on his summons 'to serve the king.' F.W. Brooks, *The Council in the North*, revised edition (1966), 7. In February 1484, John Howard, seven months earlier created duke of Norfolk, promised Richard III one thousand men. His notebooks list the names of several hundred of them and the estates from which they came, including the contingents of two knights and three or four gentlemen. Howard expected his tenants and officials to make their contributions. For example, his auditor, John Knight, promised to provide six soldiers at his own expense. *Household Books of John, Duke of Norfolk, and Thomas, Earl of Surrey, Temp. 1481–1490*, ed. J. Payne Collier (Roxburghe Club 1844), 480.

52 M.R. Powicke, 'Lancastrian Captains,' in *Essays in Medieval History Presented to Bertie Wilkinson*, ed. T.A. Sandquist and M.R. Powicke (Toronto 1969), 371–82.

53 J.R. Lander, 'The Hundred Years' War and Edward IV's 1475 Campaign in France,' in *Tudor Men and Institutions*, ed. Slavin, Baton Rouge 91–100, reprinted in Lander, *Crown and Nobility, 1450–1509*, 239–41.

54 *Calendar of State Papers and Manuscripts Existing in the Archives and Collections of Milan,* 1:340. The Venetian ambassador of 1497, though admitting that the English had a high reputation in arms, made the same point. *A Relation, or Rather a True Account of the Island of England,* 23; *Commynes,* 2:29.

55 William Worcestre, *The Boke of Noblesse,* ed. J.G. Nichols (Roxburghe Club 1860), 77–78; *The Prologues and Epilogues of William Caxton,* ed. W.J.B. Crotch (Early English Text Society 1928), 82–4.

56 K.B. McFarlane, *The Nobility of Later Medieval England* (Oxford 1973), 231–3.

57 J.R. Lander, *The Wars of the Roses* (London 1965), 21.

58 'Gregory's Chronicle,' in *The Historical Collections of a Citizen of London in the Fifteenth Century,* ed. J. Gairdner (Camden Series 1876), 190.

59 Ibid., 205.

60 C.L. Scofield, *The Life and Reign of Edward IV,* 2 vols. (London 1923), 1: 117.

61 *Historie of the Arrivall of Edward IV in England and the Finall Recouery of His Kingdomes from Henry VI, A.D. M. CCCCLXXI,* ed. J. Bruce (Camden Series 1838), 8, 33.

62 *Three Books of Polydore Vergil's English History, comprising the Reigns of Henry VI, Edward IV and Richard III from an early translation,* ed. H. Ellis (Camden Series 1844), 199.

63 J. Bagley, *Margaret of Anjou* (London n.d.) 18 n. 1. On the other hand, Coventry because of its geographical position in the midst of hostilities suffered badly. Declining already economically, between 1449 and 1485 warfare and its attendant consequences cost the city well over the enormous sum of £20,000, including between 1469 and 1471 £600 extorted by Warwick the Kingmaker and to pacify Edward IV. C. Pythian-Adams, *Desolation of a City: Coventry and the Urban Crisis of the Late Middle Ages* (Cambridge 1979), 43.

CHAPTER TWO

1 R.M. Bird, M.W. Bucovetsky, and D.K. Foot, *The Growth of Public Employment in Canada* (Toronto 1974), chapter 3 and especially pp. 30–1. I owe this reference to P. Neary.

2 These calculations are based on an estimated population in 1500 of

about two and half million. J.L. Bolton, *The Medieval English Economy, 1150–1500* (London and Totowa, NJ 1980), 65.

3 D.A.L. Morgan, 'The King's Affinity in Yorkist England,' *Transactions of the Royal Historical Society*, 5th ser., 23 (1973), 1–25; Lander, *Government and Community: England, 1450–1509*, 34–5; B.P. Wolffe, *The Crown Lands, 1461–1536* (London and New York 1970), 63.

4 British Library, Harley 433 ffs, 301–6, 317–21, 322, 336–9.

5 R.C. Palmer, *The County Courts of Medieval England, 1150–1350* (Princeton 1982), 40–5; McKisack, *The Fourteenth Century, 1307–1399*, 206–7.

6 'Liber Niger Domus Regis Edward IV,' in *A Collection of Ordinances and Regulations for the Government of the Royal Household* (Society of Antiquaries, London 1790), 45–6; Morgan, 'The King's Affinity.' For similar phenomena as late as the reign of Elizabeth I see W.T. MacCaffery, *The Shaping of the Elizabethan Regime* (Princeton 1968), 180–1.

7 The Second Anonymous Croyland Continuator in *Rerum anglicarum scriptorum veterum*, Tom. I, ed. W. Fulman (Oxford 1684), 562.

8 Fortescue, *Governance*, 152–3.

9 E.g. the case of Knaresborough, the earl of Northumberland and Sir William Plumpton, *The Plumpton Correspondence*, ed. T. Stapleton (Camden Series 1839), 31–3. During the 1460s, offices in the administration of the duchies of Lancaster and York in the West Riding of Yorkshire had been monopolized by the earl of Warwick and his brother Marquis Montague, and to these offices they appointed the lesser lawyers and esquires of the district as their deputies. These same deputies were also prominent on the commission of the peace. C. Arnold, 'The Commission of the Peace for the West Riding of Yorkshire,' in *Property and Politics: Essays in Later Medieval English History*, ed. A.J. Pollard (Gloucester, New York 1984), 126. For Lord Hastings' probable influence on the appointment of sheriffs and justices of the peace in the Midlands, see W.H. Dunham, Jr, 'Lord Hastings' Indentured Retainers. 1461–1483,' *Transactions of the Connecticut Academy of Arts and Sciences*, 39 (1955), 36–40; I. Rowney, 'Resources and Retaining in Yorkist England: William, Lord Hastings and the Honour of Tutbury,' in *Property and Politics*, 139–55. This article also demonstrates that to a very great

extent Hastings financed his famous affinity out of the royal resources and at very little cost to himself. See also J.A. Tuck, 'Richard II's System of Patronage,' in *The Reign of Richard II: Essays in Honour of May McKisack*, ed. F.R.H. Du Boulay and C.M. Barron (London 1971), 15–17. See also the examples given by Plummer in Fortescue, *Governance*, 333–6.

10 The point is strengthened by the fact that a number of prominent royal bureaucrats were also employed by magnates. R.A. Griffiths, 'Public and Private Bureaucracies in England and Wales in the Fifteenth Century,' *Transactions of the Royal Historical Society*, 5th ser., 30 (1980), 113ff. For an opposing point of view, see C. Carpenter, 'The Beauchamp Affinity: A Study of Bastard Feudalism at Work,' *English Historical Review*, 95 (1980), 519. For the importance of royal patronage in the maintenance of a local aristocratic affinity, see M. Cherry, 'The Struggle for Power in Mid-fifteenth Century Devonshire,' in *Patronage, the Crown and the Provinces in Later Medieval England*, ed. R.A. Griffiths (Gloucester, England and Atlantic Highlands, NJ 1981), 123–4.

11 J.C. Sainty, 'The Tenure of Office in the Exchequer,' *English Historical Review*, 80 (1965), 449–75; J. Otway-Ruthven, *The King's Secretary and the Signet Office in the Fifteenth Century* (Cambridge 1939), chapter 7. For the proportion of their incomes which landowners obtained from offices, see J.R. Lander, *Conflict and Stability in the Fifteenth Century England*, 3rd ed. (London 1977), 174–5. P. Williams, *The Tudor Regime* (Oxford 1979), 81–108, especially 107–8, considers that, as a result of these factors and others, 'The crown's servants in the sixteenth century were in many ways less effective as administrative instruments than had been their predecessors in the fourteenth and early fifteenth centuries.'

12 M.T. Clanchy, *From Memory to Written Record: England, 1066–1307* (London 1979), 138–47. Although Clanchy writes about an earlier period, his remarks are equally applicable later. Great efforts and some improvements do seem to have occurred in the fifteenth century, however. Under Edward IV, Exchequer officials made extensive searches for information. In the Easter Term, 3 Edward IV, the clerks of the Treasurer's Remembrancer were paid £20 for special work in compiling divers rolls of farms, wards, and marriages at

the king's disposal, and Nicholas Lathell, the Clerk of the Great
Roll, was also paid £20 for himself and his clerks 'in scrutando et
laborando in officio suo per mandatum Thesaurii Anglie in diversis
rotulis et libris tam de custumnis et subsidis temporibus regni
Edwardi Tercii, Ricardus secundi, Henrici IV, Henrici VI et Henrici
VI.' Public Record Office, Issue Roll, P.R.O., E. 403/829, ms 3 and
5. B.P. Wolffe points out that the Lancastrian Exchequer produced
frequent, possibly annual, estimates of royal financial needs and
resources and that by Richard III's time the government had drawn
up effective lists of local offices and was better informed about
these than ever before, B.P. Wolffe, *The Crown Lands, 1461 to 1536*
(London and New York 1970), 37; British Library, ms Harley 433
ff. 310–16, 317–21, 322, 336–9.

13 O. Coleman, 'What Figures: Some Thoughts on the Use of Information by Medieval Governments,' in *Trade, Government and Economy in
Pre-Industrial England: Essays Presented to F.J. Fisher*, ed. D.C. Coleman
and A.H. John (London 1976), 96–112.

14 *Annales Ricardi Secundi et Henrici Quinti*, ed. H.T. Riley (Rolls Series
1866), 379. T. Walsingham, *Historia anglicana* (Rolls Series 1863–4), 2:
260, *Rot. Parl.*, v, 211, vi, 5, 111–19, 149–53. *English Historical
Documents*, vol 4, *1327–1485*, ed. A.R. Myers (London 1969),
379–80. J.R. Lander, 'The Hundred Years' War and Edward IV's
1475 Campaign in France,' in *Tudor Men and Institutions*, ed.
Slavin, 84–89, reprinted in Lander, *Crown and Nobility, 1450–1509*,
230–4.

15 Williams, *The Tudor Regime*, 11. See also E.F. Jacob, *The Fifteenth
Century, 1399–1485* (Oxford 1961), 317, 327, J.R. Lander, 'Marriage
and Politics in the Fifteenth Century: The Nevilles and the Wydevilles,' *Bulletin of the Institute of Historical Research*, (1963), 148,
reprinted in Lander, *Crown and Nobility, 1450–1509*, 123.

16 I hope to deal with the justices of the peace in detail in a forthcoming
work.

17 There were also generally a number of bishops, abbots, priors, and
influential royal clerks on the commissions. The number of royal
clerks very much increased under Henry VII.

18 C.F. Richmond, 'Fauconberg's Kentish Rising of May, 1470,' *English
Historical Review*, 85 (1970), 673–92.

19 R.A. Griffiths, *The Reign of King Henry VI: The Exercise of Royal Authority, 1422–46* (Berkeley 1981), 329–46.

20 A.J. Pollard, 'The Tyranny of Richard III,' *Journal of Medieval History*, 3 (1977), 147–65.

21 J.E.A. Jolliffe, *Angevin Kingship* (London 1955), Introduction, chapters 3 and 4, and Recapitulation.

22 Ibid., 347.

23 See, for example, the case of Arnulph of Lisieux. Jolliffe, *Angevin Kingship*, 20 n. 3, 103–4, 107.

24 M.T. Clanchy, 'Law, Government and Society in Medieval England,' *History*, 59 (1974), 78.

25 J.R. Maddicott, *Law and Lordship: Royal Justices as Retainers in Thirteenth- and Fourteenth-Century England*, Past and Present Supplement, 4 (1978).

26 A. Harding, *The Law Courts of Medieval England*, (London and New York 1973), 90–1; R.W. Kaeuper, 'Law and Order in Fourteenth Century England: The Evidence of Special Commissions of Oyer and Terminer,' *Speculum*, 54 (1979), 735–8 and the numerous references given on 735 n. 4. For the reign of Henry IV see J.H. Wylie, *History of England under Henry IV*, 4 vols. (London 1884–98), 2: 189–90 and *Rot. Parl.*, iii, 649. During the fifteenth century there may have been some improvement, for after the reign of Henry IV there are no known complaints about the judges. J.G. Bellamy, *Crime and Public Order in England in the Later Middle Ages* (London and Toronto 1973), 14–16.

27 Kaeuper, 'Law and Order in Fourteenth Century England,' 781–4.

28 R.H.C. Davis, *King Stephen, 1135 to 1154* (London 1967), 14–16, 24, 59–60, 67–9, 121–6.

29 Joliffe, *Angevin Kingship*, chapter 3.

30 K.B. McFarlane, 'Had Edward I a "policy" towards the earls?,' *History*, 50 (1965), 145–9.

31 M. Prestwich, *The Three Edwards: War and State in England, 1272 to 1377* (London 1980), 154–5. For further deleterious developments in the fifteenth century see J.L. Barton, 'The Medieval Use,' *Law Quarterly Review*, 81 (1965), 562–77: J.M.W. Bean, *The Decline and Fall of English Feudalism, 1215 to 1540* (Manchester and New York 1968), chapters 3

and 4; E.W. Ives, 'The Genesis of the Statute of Uses,' *English Historical Review*, 82 (1967), 673–97.

32 During the greater part of his reign, Edward IV had been extremely wary of challenging powerful families, an attitude which remained as late as 1475 in his dealing with the duke of Norfolk in East Anglia. E.g. *Paston Letters and Papers of the Fifteenth Century*, ed. N. Davis (Oxford 1971) 1: 595. The families alienated during his later years were Howard, Berkeley, Buckingham, Neville (Westmorland), Talbot, and Welles and Willoughby. C. Ross, *Edward IV* (London 1974), 331ff; Lander, *Government and Community: England, 1450–1509*, 299–301.

33 M.A. Hicks, 'Descent, Partition and Extinction: The Warwick Inheritance,' *Bulletin of the Institute of Historical Research*, 52 (1979), 126ff. The accumulated Warwick inheritance consisted of the lands of four powerful magnate families, Despenser (part), Neville (part), Salisbury (Montecute), and Beauchamp. Before 1461 the earls of Salisbury and Warwick (father and son) had obtained possession of at least a large part of these estates by dubious means, blocking the rights of co-heirs by a combination of influence at the Lancastrian court and outright violence. As M.A. Hicks has pointed out, possession was enough to place Salisbury and Warwick amongst the half-dozen leading magnates. United in Warwick's hands in the 1460s, these estates made him unrivalled in power. Divided again in the 1470s between Clarence and Gloucester (the husbands of Warwick's two daughters), they made the king's brothers powerful magnates, possibly equalled only by the dukes of Buckingham and Norfolk. The turbulent political careers of Salisbury, Warwick, Clarence, and Gloucester would have been quite impossible without possession of these territories and the powerful affinities which they supported. M.A. Hicks, *Descent, Partition*, 116–28. It should, however, be pointed out that Henry VII was able to act under especially favourable circumstances. Richard III (Gloucester) died without direct heirs. Henry held the countess of Warwick (the rightful heiress of the immense Beauchamp properties) more or less a prisoner. Clarence's attainder of 1478 was still unreversed. His son, the earl of Warwick, was also prisoner until his execution on a trumped-up charge of treason in 1499. After

Warwick's death Henry could fairly easily ignore his sister
Margaret's claim to the entire inheritance. Moreover, while she was
alive her superior title barred the claims of the collateral heirs,
Lords Lisle, Roos, and Latimer, to the Beauchamp lands. It was
obviously more hazardous to ignore the claims of Lord Burgavenny,
the common-law heir of the Despenser estates. It is possible (though
this is conjecture only and cannot be proved) that Burgavenny's
notorious prosecution and colossal suspended fine for retaining in
1507 may have been in part deliberate intimidation in Henry's
scheme for fragmenting the Warwick inheritance.

34 J.R. Lander, 'Bonds, Coercion and Fear: Henry vii and the Peerage,'
in *Florilegium Historiale: Essays Presented to Wallace K. Ferguson*, ed.
J.G. Rowe and W.H. Stockdale (Toronto 1971), 327–67, reprinted in
Lander, *Crown and Nobility, 1450–1509*, 267–300.

35 Harding, *The Law Courts of Medieval England*, 94, 97–8. On the other
hand, R.A. Griffiths (*Public and Private Bureaucracies*, 128–9) argues
that the emergent class of highly professional bureaucrats (generally
themselves landowners) who staffed the royal estate bureaucracy
and the estate bureaucracies of the magnates by supplementing the
increasing deficiencies of the courts of common law were a powerful
influence in settling disputes by arbitration and reducing local feuds.

36 J.P. Dawson, *A History of Lay Judges* (Cambridge, Mass 1960), 127.

37 H.M. Cam, 'Cambridgeshire Sheriffs in the Thirteenth Century,' in
Liberties and Communities in Medieval England (Cambridge 1944),
27–48. The ideal of the reforming party in 1258 was annual appointment. The provisions of Oxford laid down that no sheriff should hold
office for more than a year. Ibid. 34.

38 D.A. Carpenter, 'The Decline of the Curial Sheriff in England,
1194–1258,' *English Historical Review*, 90 (1976), 1–32.

39 For a full discussion see R. Virgoe, 'The Crown and Local Government: East Anglia under Richard ii,' in *The Reign of Richard II: Essays in
Honour of May McKisack*, ed. F.R.H. Du Boulay and C.M. Barron
(London 1971), 218–22. As Virgoe points out, although various
petitions stress the heavy burdens and expenses borne by the
sheriffs, the attempt to extend a similar ban to the offices of escheator
and deputies 'makes it clear that the main purpose of such petitions
was to prevent the establishment of a local bureaucracy and thus

avoid excessive crown interference in local affairs.' Virgoe also points out that during the fourteenth century many of the duties of local officials were taken over by commissions appointed by the crown but composed largely of resident knights and esquires who were most likely to voice the views of their class and district. Ibid., 233.

40 Griffiths, *Henry VI*, 233, 334–6, 340. M. Condon, 'Ruling Elites in the Reign of Henry vii,' in *Patronage, Pedigree and Power in Late Medieval England*, ed. C. Ross (Gloucester and Totowa, NJ 1979), 125–6.

41 Harding, *The Law Courts of Medieval England*, 86–92.

42 Kaeuper, 'Law and Order in Fourteenth-Century England,' 734–84 and especially 781–4. Between 1275 and 1279 about 100 or more commissions a year were issued, followed by a fall in the 1280s and 1290s. A peak of 270 commissions was reached in 1318, followed by a similar peak in 1327. By the mid-thirties they had fallen to less than 120 and from the forties they steadily declined to between 20 and 40 or even less by the seventies. More general commissions of oyer and terminer were, of course, always issued, and in the fifteenth century Edward iv, in particular, made extensive use of them. Lander, *Conflict and Stability in Fifteenth Century England*, 98.

43 Lack of space precludes discussion of all the expedients involved – for example, the notorious commissions of trailbaston. For the contents of this paragraph, see B.H. Putnam, 'The Transformation of the Keepers of the Peace into Justices of the Peace,' *Transactions of the Royal Historical Society*, 4th ser., 12 (1929), 19–48. Harding, *The Law Courts of Medieval England*, 94–8.

44 He was extremely hostile to the keepers of the peace and their transformation into justices (see below pp. 30ff.). C.H. Putnam, *The Place in Legal History of Sir William Shareshull* (Cambridge 1950), 60.

45 That is officials authorized to receive but not to determine indictments. They had a long pre-history in the thirteenth century: see A. Harding, 'The Origins and Early History of the Keeper of the Peace,' *Transactions of the Royal Historical Society*, 5th ser., 10 (1960), 85–109, and B.H. Putnam, 'Shire Officials: Keepers of the Peace and Justices of the Peace,' in the *English Government at Work, 1327 to 1336*, ed. J.F. Willard, W.A. Morris, and W.H. Dunham, Jr, vol. 3, *Local Administration and Justice* (Medieval Academy of America 1950), 185–217.

46 Extensions of their jurisdictions soon followed; e.g., responsibility for the enforcement of wage regulations and other economic matters, and the regulation of morals.

47 For the contents of this paragraph see R.L. Storey, 'Liveries and Commissions of the Peace, 1388 to 1390,' in *The Reign of Richard II: Essays in Honour of May McKisack*, ed. Du Boulay and Barron, 131–52, and R. Virgoe, 'The Crown and Local Government: East Anglia under Richard II,' in ibid., 218–41.

48 R. Virgoe, 'The Crown, Magnates and Local Government in Fifteenth Century East Anglia,' in *The Crown and Local Communities in England and France in the Fifteenth Century*, ed. J.R.L. Highfield and R. Jeffs (Gloucester 1981), 72.

49 *Rot. Parl.*, v, 28.

50 See above pp. 22–3 and nn. 8, 9, and 10.

51 W.H. Dunham, Jr, 'Lord Hastings' Indentured Retainers, 1461–1483,' *Transactions of the Connecticut Academy of Arts and Sciences*, 39 (1955), 37–40; M. Cherry, 'The Courtenay Earls of Devon: The Formation and Disintegration of a Late Medieval Aristocratic Affinity,' *Southern History*, 1 (1979), 71–97; A.J. Pollard, 'The Northern Retainers of Richard Nevill, Earl of Salisbury,' *Northern History*, 11 (1976 for 1975), 52–69. J.A. Tuck, 'Northumbrian Society in the Fourteenth Century,' *Northern History*, 6 (1971), 39, states the traditional view that the men of the north 'would have no other lord but a Percy,' but M. Weiss, 'A Power in the North? The Percies in the Fifteenth Century,' *Historical Journal*, 19 (1976), 501–9, and M.A. Hicks, 'Dynastic Change and Northern Society: The Career of the Fourth Earl of Northumberland,' *Northern History*, 14 (1978), especially 101–3, deny this interpretation, stressing instead that the decline of Percy influence during the late fifteenth century was partly due to instability caused by successive dynastic revolutions at the centre and to what their followers regarded as increasingly inadequate lordship, and partly due to royal interference. See also M.E. James, 'The First Earl of Cumberland and the Decline of Northern Feudalism,' *Northern History*, 1 (1966), 43–69. Affinities, particularly when some of the members were powerful men in their own right, could get out of hand and perhaps go beyond the wishes of their lords. See the case of the Devereux-Herbert gang (part of Richard of York's affinity) in

'Herefordshire, 1413–1461: Some Aspects of Society and Public Order,' in *Patronage, the Crown and the Provinces in Later Medieval England*, ed. R.A. Griffiths (Gloucester, England and Atlantic Highlands, NJ 1981), 103–22.

52 In Norfolk and Suffolk between 1399 and 1450 the commissions fluctuated between twelve and seventeen with a slight tendency to increase. There was a notable increase during the 1450s and during the Yorkist period. The average membership of the Norfolk commission increased from something under sixteen to over twenty-four and the Suffolk commission to over twenty. By the 1480s the numbers were to increase to around thirty and after 1500 rarely fell below that level. The increase in size came mainly from the addition of resident knights and esquires. Information from R. Virgoe, 'The Crown, Magnates and Local Government in East Anglia,' 78–9. For the whole country (with wide variations county to county) the average increase was from fifteen in 1439 to twenty-five in 1509. J.C. Wedgwood, *History of Parliament, 1439 to 1509*, 2 vols. (London 1936, 1938), *Register*, lvii.

53 I hope to provide detailed evidence for these points in a forthcoming work on the justices of the peace between 1461 and 1509. For Richard III's intrusion of northern followers into southern commissions, see above p. 25 and n. 20.

54 J.B. Aurutic, 'Commissions of Oyer and Terminer in Fifteenth Century England,' unpublished M PHIL dissertation, University of London 1976. Lander, *Conflict and Stability in Fifteenth Century England*, 98. Virgoe's researches referred to above in n. 48 also confirm this for East Anglia.

55 E.g. H.M. Cam, 'The Decline and Fall of English Feudalism,' *History*, 25 (1940), 216–33, especially 225. Reprinted in *Liberties and Communities in Medieval England* (Cambridge 1944), 205–22, especially 214. See also Lander, *Crown and Nobility, 1450–1509*, 8–11.

56 G.A. Holmes, *The Estates of the Higher Nobility in Fourteenth Century England* (Cambridge 1957), 83–4. W.H. Dunham, Jr, 'Lord Hastings' Indentured Retainers, 1461–1483,' chapter 5.

57 See cases of John Newport and George Neville, duke of Bedford, *Rot. Parl.*, v, 204–5, vi, 173. For property qualifications for justices of the peace and certain types of jurors, *Rot. Parl.*, v, 28, *Statute Roll*, 1

Richard III, c. 4. For the corruption of court officials and for dislike of poorer men as jurors and court suitors, *Rot. Parl.*, v, 267, 493–4. Also the duchy of Lancaster ordinances c. 1482: 'Also the said particular stiwardes or their deputies shall calle to every lete or grete courtes all the homagiers thereof, and *most specially* the gentilmen to appere in thair owne persons, and charge them oonly with the presentementes of the defaultes of the said court, *by cause of thay be excused and the homagiers oonly chosen of the pour men, then the said pour men dare not present the said defaultes as they shuld do, to the Kynges grete hurt and to the dishonnour of the said court.*' 'Also that the Sherif and Undersherif, Coroners and othir clerks and elusours also of the said countie for the tyme being charged and openly sworne, in plain session bifore the Justices at Lancastre and other of the Kinges Counseill there, to empanell knightes and squiers and the most sufficiaunt men of lyvelode within the said countie in enquestes both for the king and for the parties, not letting neither for lucre nor for affeccion, drede ne love of any person, and that they empannel in semble wise byfore the Justicz of the pees ther.' 'Ordinances for the Duchy of Lancaster,' ed. Sir R. Somerville, *Camden Miscellany*, 26 (1975), 17, 29.

58 'Ffor the myght of þe lande, *aftir* the myght of þe grete lordes þeroff, stondith most in þe kynges officers. Ffor thai mowe best rule þe countreis wher as þer offices ben, wich is euery partie of the lande. A pouere baylyff mey do more in his bayille *than any man of his degre* dewllyge with in his office. Some fforester of the kynges, that hath non oþer livelod, mey brynge moo men to þe felde well areyed, and namely ffor shotynge, then may some knyght or Squyer off ryght gret lyuelode, dwellyne be hym, and hauynge non offyce.' Fortescue, *Governance*, 151.

59 In addition to his numerous household and estate officials Gaunt's permanent retinue (as distinct from that raised for individual campaigns) consisted of at least two peers, twenty-nine knights, and forty-two esquires, and the records may well be incomplete. *John of Gaunt's Register*, ed. S. Armitage-Smith, 2 vols. (Camden Series 1911) 2, nos. 775–80.

60 A.L. Brown, 'The Reign of Henry IV: The Establishment of the Lancastrian Regime,' in *Fifteenth Century England, 1399–1509: Studies in Politics and Society*, ed. S.B. Chrimes, C.D. Ross, and R.A.

Griffiths, 1–25. Also T.B. Pugh, 'The Magnates, Knights and Gentry,' 107–8.

61 *Rot. Parl.*, iii, 524–5. For the background of this episode see W. Stubbs, *The Constitutional History of England*, 3 (1878), 41.

62 Jolliffe, *Angevin Kingship*, 348.

63 Pugh, 'The Magnates, Knights and Gentry,' 108–9.

64 K.B. McFarlane, 'The Wars of the Roses' *Proceedings of the British Academy*, 50 (1964), 92–4.

65 Between 1448 and 1455 the dukes of Exeter and Norfolk, the earls of Devon and Wiltshire, Lords Bonvile, Cobham, Cromwell, Egremont, Grey, Moleyns, and Say. R.L. Storey, *The End of the House of Lancaster* (London 1966), 79 and appendix IV, 'John Benet's Chronicle for the Years 1400–1462.' ed. G.L. Harriss, *Camden Miscellany*, 9 (1972), 199–217. In 1450 York had also imprisoned the duke of Somerset in the Tower of London, ostensibly for his own safety.

66 Lander, *Crown and Nobility, 1450–1509*, 20–2, 24–5 and appendices A and B.

67 McFarlane, 'The Wars of the Roses,' 117–18.

68 Sir Frances Bacon, *The History of the Reign of King Henry VII*, ed. R. Lockyer (Folio Society 1971), 233.

69 J.R. Lander, 'Bonds, Coercion and Fear: Henry VII and the Peerage,' in *Florilegium Historiale: Essays Presented to Wallace K. Ferguson*, ed. Rowe and Stockdale, 327–67, reprinted in Lander, *Crown and Nobility, 1450–1509*, 267–300.

70 E.g. see Pythian-Adams, *Desolation of a city*, Part III.

71 Lander, *Goverment and Community: England, 1450–1509*, 35–6.

72 J.R. Lander, 'The Yorkist Council, Justice and Public Order: The Case of Straunge versus Kynaston,' *Albion*, 12 (1980), 7.

73 J.B. Bellamy, 'Justice under the Yorkist Kings,' *American Journal of Legal History*, 9 (1965), 135–55.

74 J. Otway-Ruthven, 'The Constitutional Position of the Great Lordships of South Wales,' *Transactions of the Royal Historical Society*, 5th ser., 8 (1958), 1–20; Lander, *Crown and Nobility, 1450–1509*, 23, 207–8; Ross, 'The Reign of Edward IV,' in *Fifteenth Century England, 1399–1509: Studies in Politics and Society*, 56.

75 Dunham, *Lord Hastings' Indentured Retainers*, 33–46, J.A. Guy, *The Cardinal's Court: The Impact of Thomas Wolsey in Star Chamber* (Hassocks, England 1977), 121.

76 Williams, *The Tudor Regime*, 5.
77 *Rot. Parl.*, v, 181–2; E.F. Jacob, *The Fifteenth Century, 1399–1485* (Oxford 1961), 492–3. R.L. Storey, *The End of the House of Lancaster* (London 1966), appendix III.
78 Ross, 'The Reign of Edward IV,' in *Fifteenth Century England: Studies in Politics and Society, 1399 to 1509*, 59. Gloucester's exercise of lordship in Wales was also generous. Although T.B. Pugh considers that this can be seen partly as an attempt at administrative reform, he admits that as such it was unsuccessful. T.B. Pugh, 'The Marcher Lordships of Glamorgan and Morgannwg, 1317–1485,' in *The Glamorgan County History*, vol. 3, *The Middle Ages*, ed. T.B. Pugh (Cardiff 1971), 202–3.
79 J.A. Guy, *The Cardinal's Court: The Impact of Thomas Wolsey in Star Chamber*, 121.
80 See Pugh, 'The Marcher Lordships, especially 202–4, and 'The Ending of the Middle Ages, 1485–1536,' 555–81; R.A. Griffiths, *The Principality of Wales in the Later Middle Ages, vol. 1, South Wales, 1297–1536* (Cardiff 1972), 27–33, 56–7, 68–9.
81 Lander, *Conflict and Stability in Fifteenth Century England*, 167–8.
82 M. Hastings, *The Court of Common Pleas in Fifteenth Century England* (Ithaca, NY 1947), chapter 15; M. Blatcher, *The Court of King's Bench, 1450–1550: A Study in Self-Help* (London 1978), chapters 4 and 5.
83 C. Rawcliffe, 'Baronial Councils in the Later Middle Ages,' in *Patronage, Pedigree and Power in Later Medieval England*, ed. C. Ross (Gloucester, England, and Totowa, NJ 1979), 91–3. C. Carpenter, 'The Beauchamp Affinity: A Study of Bastard Feudalism at Work,' *English Historical Review* 95 (1980), 530–1.
84 *The Paston Letters*, ed. J. Gairdner, 4 vols. (Edinburgh 1910), 1: 233. See also ibid., 3: 53–54.
85 See K.B. McFarlane, 'Parliament and "Bastard Feudalism",' *Transactions of the Royal Historical Society*, 4th ser., 26 (1944), 63–73; C. Rawcliffe, 'Baronial Councils,' 87–8. The Venetian envoy of 1497 saw this as a weakness, commenting that the English aristocracy's lack of formal judicial powers (a consequence of the scattering of their estates) was to a great extent responsible for the appalling level of crime in England. *A Relation or Rather a True Account of the Island of England*, ed. Sneyd, 34, 36.
86 J.M.W. Bean, *The Estates of the Percy Family, 1416 to 1537* (Oxford 1958), 85–98.

87 M.A. Hicks, 'Dynastic Change and Northern Society: The Career of the Fourth Earl of Northumberland,' *Northern History*, 14 (1978), 78–107.

88 T.B. Pugh, *The Marcher Lordships of South Wales, 1415–1536*, Board of Celtic Studies History and Law Series, 20 (1963), 239–61. Edward's father, Duke Henry (died 1483), seems to have been equally unpopular. *Three Books of Polydore Vergil's English History, comprising the Reigns of Henry VI, Edward IV and Richard III*, ed. Sir H. Ellis (Camden Series 1844), 199. The Vaughans of Tretower had a history of more than fifty years' service with the Stafford family, but in 1483 as soon as the duke left Brecon Castle they sacked it and burned its contents. H. Owen and J.B. Blakeway, *A History of Shrewsbury*, 2 vols. (London 1825), 1: 235–42.

CHAPTER THREE

1 T.A. Sandquist, 'The Holy Oil of St Thomas of Canterbury,' in *Essays in Medieval History presented to Bertie Wilkinson*, ed. T.A. Sandquist and M.R. Powicke (Toronto 1969), 330–44. W. Ullman, 'Thomas Becket's Miraculous Oil,' *Journal of Theological Studies*, new ser., 8 (1937), 129–33. Ullman attributes much greater significance to the holy oil in the fifteenth century than does Sandquist, who rather downgrades its importance for the Lancastrian dynasty.

2 Henry vi also created d'Almada duke of Avranches. The manuscript must have been written before 1449, as the count was then killed at the battle of Altarobeia in Portugal and the manuscript describes him as still living. *Liber regie capelle*, ed. W. Ullman, Bradshaw Society, 92 (Cambridge 1961), 9–11.

3 Ullman notes that the suggestion that Charles v's personal copy of the *ordo* came into the hands of the duke of Bedford after 1425 'has everything in its favour.' Ullman, 29.

4 Ibid., 22ff. Ullman comments that this would also strengthen the significance of the first clause of the coronation oath with its emphasis on the *donum dei* idea of kingship as against the constitutional emphasis of the fourth clause (first introduced at the coronation of Edward ii), which implied that as well as the laws granted by the king 'there is the written and unwritten law which is the expres-

sion of the consent and of approval by both king and community of the realm.' Ibid., 32.

5 Ibid., 41.

6 Ibid., 39. Ullman points out that under Philip IV of France the French Estates General, unlike the English parliament, were summoned *ad obedientum* and French laws were issued *de plentitude regie potestas*. Ullman, 39 n. 1. In 1527 the Parliament of Paris told Francis I: 'We know well that you are above the laws and that the laws and ordinances cannot constrain you ... ' P.S. Lewis, *Later Medieval France: The Polity* (London and New York 1968), 87.

7 Information from a paper, 'Patronage and Propaganda in Medieval English Art: The Decoration of Royal and Private Charters,' given by E.A. Danbury at the Anglo-American Conference of Historians, 5 July 1985.

8 J.R. Lander, 'Marriage and Politics in the Fifteenth Century: The Nevilles and the Wydevilles,' *Bulletin of the Institute of Historical Research*, 36 (1963), 128–9, reprinted in Lander, *Crown and Nobility, 1450–1509*, 103–4.

9 *Rot. Parl.*, v, 375–80.

10 C.A.J. Armstrong, 'The Inauguration Ceremonies of the Yorkist Kings and Their Titles to the Throne,' *Transactions of the Royal Historical Society*, 4th ser., 30 (1948), 53–4.

11 Ibid., 55–6.

12 Ibid., 48–67. For the development of 'lauds' see E.H. Kantorowicz, *Laudes Regiae: A Study in Liturgical Acclamations and Medieval Ruler Worship* (Berkeley and Los Angeles 1958), chapters 1–4 and 6.

13 R.L. Storey, 'Gentlemen-bureaucrats' in *Profession, Vocation and Culture in Later Medieval England: Essays Dedicated to the Memory of A.R. Myers*, ed. C.H. Clough (Liverpool 1982), 90–129; J.-P. Genet, 'Ecclesiastics and Political Theory in Late Medieval England: The End of a Monopoly,' in *The Church, Political and Patronage in the Fifteenth Century*, ed. B. Dobson (Gloucester and New York 1984), 34.

14 R.F. Green, *Poets and Princepleasers: Literature and the English Court in the Late Middle Ages* (Toronto 1980), 182–90.

15 J.H. Fisher, 'Chancery and the Emergence of Standard Written English in the Fifteenth Century,' *Speculum*, 52 (1977), 870–99; M. Richardson, 'Henry v, the English Chancery, and Chancery English,'

Speculum, 55 (1980), 726–50; C. Ross, 'Rumour, Propaganda and Popular Opinion during the Wars of the Roses,' in *Patronage, the Crown and the Provinces in Later Medieval England*, ed. R.A. Griffiths (Gloucester, England and Atlantic Highlands, NJ 1981), 15–32.

16 J.W. McKenna, 'Henry vi of England and the Dual Monarchy: Aspects of Political Propaganda, 1422 to 1432,' *Journal of the Warburg and Courtauld Institutes*, 28 (1965), 149–50.

17 Green, *Poets and Princepleasers*, 173.

18 Ibid., 192–3.

19 Ibid., 169–71.

20 A. Allan, 'Yorkist Propaganda: Pedigree, Prophecy and the British History in the Reign of Edward iv,' in *Patronage, Pedigree and Power in Later Medieval England*, 171–8. These genealogies had Lancastrian precedents. For contemporary stress upon dynasticism see also R.A. Griffiths, 'The Sense of Dynasty in the Reign of Henry vi,' in the same volume, 13–36.

21 Allan, 'Yorkist Propaganda,' 178–88.

22 Armstrong, 'Inauguration Ceremonies,' 63–64. *Rot. Parl.*, v, 463–7.

23 *Rot. Parl.*, v, 462–3.

24 *Rot. Parl.*, v, 241.

25 G. Matthew, *The Court of Richard II* (London 1968), chapters 1 and 2.

26 A.R. Myers, *The Household of Edward IV* (Manchester 1959), 86.

27 C. Hilbert, *Agincourt* (London 1964), 110.

28 Ullman, 18.

29 Ibid., 19.

30 *The Great Chronicle of London*, ed. A.H. Thomas and I.D. Thornley (London 1938), 215.

31 In 1445 the Angevin ambassador, Antoine de la Sale (hardly a man to be easily impressed), called the English 'the most ceremonious people in matters of decorum that I have ever seen.' C.A. Knudson, 'Antoine de la Sale's Voyage to England,' *Romance Philology*, 2 (1948–9), 91. See also below n. 32.

32 The phrase is that of R.A. Griffiths, *Henry VI*, 315, 488–9. The wedding festivities cost no less than £5,129.2.0. A.R. Myers, 'The Household of Queen Margaret of Anjou,' *Bulletin of the John Rylands Library*, 40 (1957–8), 80. See also B.P. Wolffe, *Henry VI* (London 1981), 11–12.

33 Fulman, Croyland Continuator, 563. Contrast Louis xi of France, whom contemporaries derided for his shabby old felt hat with a cheap lead figure of the Virgin pinned on it, and the occasion in 1473 when the Burgundians were deeply offended by the Emperor Frederick iii's mean entourage and poor clothes. Commynes, *Mémoires*, 1: 144, 319.

34 Public Record Office, Issue Roll, p.r.o., e. 403/835, ms. 7–11.

35 *The Travels of Leo of Rozmital*, ed. M. Letts, Hakluyt Society, 2nd ser., 108 (London 1957), 5, 47.

36 Raffaelo de Negra in a letter to Bianca Maria Visconti, duchess of Milan, in 1458 wrote: 'When the wife of the Duke of Petro a Baylito, the king's son and all the duchesses speak to the queen they always go on their knees before her.' *Calendar of State Papers Milanese*, 19.

37 E.g. the reception of the Seigneur de la Gruthuyse. 'The Record of Bluemantle Pursuivant,' in C.L. Kingsford, *English Historical Literature in the Fifteenth Century* (Oxford 1913), 386–7, for the magnificence of the English champion, Lord Scales, at Margaret of York's marriage. A.B. Ferguson, *The Indian Summer of English Chivalry* (Durham, nc 1960), 19.

38 Elizabeth's mother, Jacquetta of Luxembourg, whose first husband was Henry v's brother, John, duke of Bedford, had commanded the attendence of one hundred Burgundian knights at her coronation in 1464. G. Kipling, *The Triumph of Honour: Burgundian Origins of the Elizabethan Renaissance* (Leiden 1977), 12.

39 *Mémoires d'Oliver de la Marche*, ed. H. Beaune and J. d'Arbaumont (Paris 1883–8), 4:1ff, 153–7.

40 His household cost about £14,000 a year; in comparison, that of Edward iv cost about £11,000 annually, and the ill-run household of Henry vi cost at times over £24,000. Griffiths, *Henry VI*, 319. The author of the *Black Book of the Household* (of Edward iv) wrote that a king ought to be magnificent 'circa sumptuosas expensas in quibus excellet liberalitatem.' Myers, *The Household of Edward IV*, 86.

41 For a description of his extremely rich clothing and jewels in September 1497, see the report of the Milanese ambassador, Raimondo De'Raimondi. *Calendar of State Papers and Manuscripts Existing in the Archives and Collections of Milan*, 322.

42 For early Tudor propaganda and magnificence see S. Anglo, *Spectacle, Pageantry and Early Tudor Policy* (Oxford 1969), chapters 1 to 3 and especially pp. 103–8. Also review by M. MacLagan in *English Historical Review*, 85 (1970), 575ff. L. Stone, *Sculpture in Britain: The Middle Ages* (London 1955), 229; W.C. Leedy, Jr, *Fan Vaulting: A Study of Form, Technology and Meaning* (London 1980), 32–5; P. Williams, *The Tudor Regime* (Oxford 1979), 363–4. For the courts of Henry VIII and Elizabeth I see J.E. Neale, *Queen Elizabeth* (London 1938), 67; A.L. Rowse, *The England of Elizabeth* (London 1951), 265–6; and J.H. Elliot, *Europe Divided, 1559–1598* (London 1968), 70.

43 For the contents of his paragraph see Kipling, *The Triumph of Honour: Burgundian Origins of the Elizabethan Renaissance*, especially chapters 1 to 5 and appendix 1.

44 Ibid., 3. The sum of £15,000 covered only the cost of the basic structure.

45 D. Knowles, *The Religious Orders in England* 3 vols (Cambridge 1948–59), 2: 363.

46 Lander, *Government and Community: England, 1450–1509*, 63–4.

47 Many statutes were made valid only until the following parliament, e.g. those against jurors giving untrue verdicts (1495), *Statute Roll*, c. 24, and those against false verdicts (1503), ibid., c. 3. In 1488–9 an act against the negligence of justices of the peace was to last for two years only. Ibid., c. 12.

48 Finieux wrote: 'The prince's prerogative and the subjects' privileges are solid felicities together and but empty notions asunder. That people is beyond precedent free and beyond comparison happy who restrain not the sovereign's power so far as to do them harm, as he hath none left to do them good.' Quoted in H. Maynard Smith, *Pre-Reformation England* (London 1938), 183. For the problem in general see Chrimes, *Henry VII*, chapter 8.

49 J. de Lloyd Guth, 'Exchequer Penal Law Enforcement, 1485 to 1509,' unpublished University of Pittsburg PHD thesis, 1967.

50 J.R. Green, *History of the English People*, 2 (London 1878), book v and especially pp. 27–8.

51 Ross, *Edward IV*, 247–9, 335–6; Lander, *Government and Community: England, 1450–1509*, 299–301. For avarice, 'The Lament for the Soul of Edward IV,' British Library, ms. Additional 29729 f. 85,

quoted in V.J. Scattergood, *Politics and Poetry in the Fifteenth Century* (New York 1972), 209.

52 See above p. 25 and n. 20.

53 Not only the murder of his nephews but also suspicion of murdering his queen. The Second Anonymous Croyland Continuator in Fulman, 572; *Acts of Court of the Mercers' Company, 1453–1527*, ed. L. Lyell and F.D. Watney (Cambridge 1936), 173–4.

54 For the nobility see above p. 35 and n. 69. Other groups were also subjected to the system of recognizances. These need further investigation. For contemporary condemnation of Henry's activities see *Opus Epistolarum Des, Erasmi Rotterdami*, ed. P.S. Allen, 12 vols. (1906–58), 1: 215; the 'Carmen Congratulatorium' of Sir Thomas More quoted in E.E. Reynolds, *Thomas More and Erasmus* (London 1965), 65, 145; and C.J. Harrison, 'The Petition of Edmund Dudley,' *English Historical Review*, 87 (1972), 82–99. For Henry's totally arbitrary proceedings on feudal tenures, see E.W. Ives, 'The Genesis of the Statute of Uses,' ibid., 82 (1967), 673–97.

55 H. Rashdall, *The Universities of Europe in the Middle Ages*, ed. F.M. Powicke and A.B. Emden, 3 vols (Oxford 1936), 3: 96.

56 C.I. Hammer, Jr, 'Patterns of Homicide in Fourteenth Century Oxford,' *Past and Present*, 78 (1978), 11–13.

57 *The Paston Letters*, 2:42, 53–4.

58 'It [Henry VII's government] perhaps suggests, too, a certain superficiality of achievement despite all the auguries of change: an impermanence, a fragility caused in part by the tensions which Henry VII himself created in binding and dividing the ruling elites themselves.' M.M. Condon, 'Ruling Elites in the Reign of Henry VII,' in *Patronage, Pedigree and Power in Later Medieval England*, 134.

59 Lander, *Government and Community: England, 1450–1509*, 368, quoted from Morgan, *The King's Affinity*, 17.

60 R.L. Storey, *The End of the House of Lancaster* (London 1966), 21.

61 G.R. Elton, *Policy and Police: The Enforcement of the Reformation in the Age of Thomas Cromwell* (Cambridge 1972), chapter 1, especially pp. 45–54. Elton sums up England as 'a country always hard to control and impossible to police efficiently.'

62 R.L. Storey, 'Lincolnshire and the Wars of the Roses,' *Nottingham Medieval Studies*, 14 (1970), 64–83; Lander, *Government and Com-*

munity: England 1450–1509, 257ff. See M.E. James, 'Obedience and Dissent in Henrician England: The Lincolnshire Rebellion 1536,' *Past and Present*, 48 (1970), especially 38–51. See also B.W. Beckingsale, 'The Characteristics of the Tudor North,' *Northern History*, 4 (1969), 72: 'Percy patronage was no more anarchical than Tudor patronage. The appearance of feudal unrest in the north resulted more from royal initiative than from any exercise of feudal independence. With their chosen henchmen the Tudors injected their own royal interest into the power struggle of local families and so created the illusion of feudal strife in the North.'

Index

The Joanne Goodman Lectures

1976
C.P. Stacey *Mackenzie King and the Atlantic Triangle* (Toronto: Macmillan of Canada / Maclean Hunter Press 1976)

1977
Robin W. Winks *The Relevance of Canadian History: US and Imperial Perspectives* (Toronto: Macmillan of Canada 1979)

1978
Robert Rhodes James 'Britain in Transition'

1979
Charles Ritchie 'Diplomacy: The Changing Scene'

1980
Kenneth A. Lockridge *Settlement and Unsettlement in Early America: The Crisis of Political Legitimacy before the Revolution* (New York: Cambridge University Press 1981)

1981
Geoffrey Best *Honour among Men and Nations: Transformations of an Idea* (Toronto: University of Toronto Press 1982)

1982
Carl Berger *Science, God, and Nature in Victorian Canada* (Toronto: University of Toronto Press 1983)

1983
Alistair Horne *The French Army and Politics, 1870–1970* (London: Macmillan 1984)

1984
William Freehling 'Crisis United States Style: A Comparison of the American Revolutionary and Civil Wars'

1985
Desmond Morton *Winning the Second Battle: Canadian Veterans and the Return to Civilian Life 1915–1930* (published with Glenn Wright as joint author, Toronto: University of Toronto Press 1987)

1986
J.R. Lander *The Limitations of the English Monarchy in the Later Middle Ages* (Toronto: University of Toronto Press 1988)

1987
Elizabeth Fox-Genovese 'The Female Self in the Age of Bourgeois Individualism'

1988
J.L. Granatstein 'How British Economic and Political Weakness forced Canada into the Arms of the United States: A Melodrama in Three Acts'